Brilliance

2008 Poetry Collection

Published by
The America Library of Poetry
P.O. Box 978
Houlton, ME 04730
Website: www.libraryofpoetry.com
Email: generalinquiries@libraryofpoetry.com

Printed in the United States of America

THE AMERICA
LIBRARY OF POETRY

ISBN-10   0-9773662-3-5
ISBN-13   978-0-9773662-3-1

Contents

Poetry by Division

We Shall Never Forget

Many selections in this book are dedicated to you ...
the brave men and women of America's Armed Forces
who, since that fateful day on 9/11,
have tirelessly defended your country
and who, with the love and support of your families,
continue to proudly serve here at home
and in foreign lands around the world.
It is your sacrifice and dedication
which keeps the United States of America strong and free,
and for this, we are forever in your debt.
We want you to know that we are proud of you,
that we love you,
and that we pray for you ...
and for peace.

Foreword

There are two kinds of writers in the world.
There are those who write from experience,
and those who write from imagination.
The experienced, offer words that are a reflection of their lives.
The triumphs they have enjoyed, the heartaches they have endured;
all the things that have made them who they are,
they graciously share with us, as a way of sharing themselves,
and in doing so, give us, as readers, someone to whom we may relate,
as well as fresh new perspectives
on what may be our common circumstances in life.
From the imaginative, come all the wonderful things we have yet to experience;
from sights unseen, to sounds unheard.
They encourage us to explore the limitless possibilities of our dreams and fantasies,
and aid us in escaping, if only temporarily,
the confines of reality and the rules of society.
To each, we owe a debt of gratitude;
and rightfully so, as each provides a service of equal importance.
Yet, without the other, neither can be truly beneficial.
For instance, one may succeed in accumulating a lifetime of experience,
only to consider it all to have been predictable and unfulfilling,
if denied the chance to chase a dream or two along the way.
Just as those whose imaginations run away with them, never to return,
may find, that without solid footing in the real world, life in fantasyland is empty.
As you now embark, dear reader,
upon your journey through these words to remember,
you are about to be treated to both heartfelt tales of experience,
and captivating adventures of imagination.
It is our pleasure to present them for your enjoyment.
To our many authors,
who so proudly represent the two kinds of writers in the world,
we dedicate this book, and offer our sincere thanks;
for now, possibly more than ever,
the world needs you both.

Paul Wilson Charles
Editor

Editor's Choice Award

The Editor's Choice Award is presented
to the author who,
more than any other, in our opinion,
demonstrates not only
the solid fundamentals of creative writing,
but also the ability to illicit an emotional response
or provide a thought provoking body of work
in a manner which is both clear and concise.

You will find "Who's That?"
by Veronica Biblarz
on page 199 of Brilliance

2008
Spirit of Education
For Outstanding Participation

Copper Basin
K-8 School
Queen Creek, Arizona

*Presented to participating students and faculty
in recognition of your commitment
to literary excellence.*

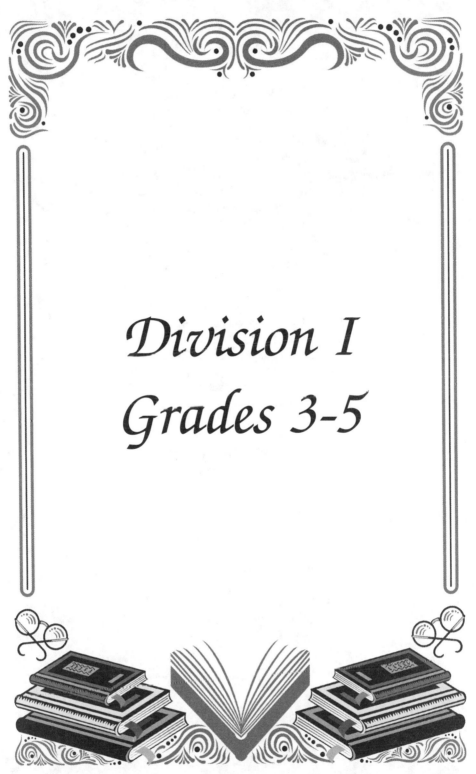

Division I
Grades 3-5

Alma
by Alma Mamani

Alma
Excited, smart, medium, happy
Enjoys soccer, my bird, and Goosebumps
Who feels good, excited, and happy
Who needs her bird, TV, and oxygen
Who gives presents, hugs, and toys
Who fears Manchester United losing, loss of candy, and Yasmin
Who would like to travel, go sledding, and go to Las Vegas, Nevada
Resident of Pennsylvania
Mamani

Cows
by Ashley Bradley

I know a cow named Buff
He had a friend named Puff
He could be heard from a mile away
At the bank he had to pay
He went to school
And his dad was a bull

Dark Night
by Leta Cirigliano

Dark as the nightfall
You fall so far you cannot be tall or small
Tiptoe as the night shall fall
Slow and quiet as you know
Cats and bats entering your path
As you step away
You see the moon above your head
You tiptoe along crying
While wishing you were in bed at nightfall

Horses Are Amazing
by Jessica Sun

Look at that horse neigh and eat hay
Just look at that horse galloping that way
It takes people where they need to go
By carriage, by sled, any way you choose
They come in different colors
White, brown, and black
They even come in chestnut
Some of them are two colors
There are so many types of horses
Wild horses, and horses you can have as pets
And train them too
Just look at all the things that horses can do
Every single horse is unique in their own unique way
That's how horses are amazing

Faces of Freedom
by Kayleigh Dean

When I think of faces of freedom
I think of Abraham Lincoln
He let slaves go free
And he worked hard for their freedom
When I think of faces of freedom
I think of George Washington
He led the Revolutionary War
To gain our freedom from Britain
When I think of faces of freedom
I think of the Statue of Liberty
That symbol lets people know
That they are welcome to our country
And they will have freedom

Faces of Freedom
by Faith Shoemaker

George Washington was our country's first face of freedom
After he led our country to victory in the Revolutionary War
He became our first president
I see the Statue of Liberty as a face of freedom
I wish I could be in New York City
Where she could be looking at me
The Liberty Bell is another symbol of our freedom
Many people's faces smiled when they heard the ring
It was the song of being free

Book Bonanza
by Hannah Neiderhiser

Oh books, oh books
With pages so full
What wonders await me?
I do not know
With genres of all sorts
With lessons and themes
While I'm reading a book
I can be anything!
With point of view
And main character, too
I can go anywhere
Even to Neptune!

Faces of Freedom
by Bryan R. Johnson

When I think of faces of freedom, I think of soldiers
Because they made the U.S.A. a free country
Another face I think of is Martin Luther King, Jr.
Because he helped all kinds of people get equal rights
The third face I think of is George Washington
Because he led the Revolutionary War and freed our country

My Window
by Kristianna Beyschau

As I look out my window
And far down the street
I think of all the people
Who tread it with their feet
My window is a one way portal
To my outside world
People aren't looking back at me
Or so I'm told
When I look out my window
Clean, shiny, and clear
In my sanctuary quiet
I can't hear what they hear
As far as I can tell
As far as I can see
My one true friend
My window and me

Horsing Around
by Gina Johnston

On my birthday, many years ago
My mom asked me what I wanted
It was a birthday you see
I had simply one reply
I want a horse of course you see
The horse is the pet for me
No Clydesdales or miniature ponies
I want a quarter horse
They clip and clop
They never stop
Prancing through the fields
A few years later
About right now
I'm still trying to convince
A horse is the pet for me!

Summer Vacation
by Alaina Stewart

I'm on a summer vacation
It's just you and me
I'm on a summer vacation
Riding an ATV
I'm on a summer vacation
Riding on the waves
I'm on a summer vacation
Missing two school days

Ben
by Ben Lincoln

Ben
Crazy, funny, jumpy, hungry
Brother of Grant
Enjoys PS2, TV and Xbox 360
Who feels crazy, happy when I'm near my brother, hungry
Who needs video games, TV and movies
Who gives help, video games and money
Who fears Jason in horror movies, sky diving, and Freddy Krueger
Who would like to travel, get video games, play PS2
Resident of Pennsylvania
Lincoln

Courtney
by Tesla London

Courtney is a nice girl
She always has a nice thrill
She likes frogs
She has no hogs
Courtney is not a squirrel

Rebecca
by Rebecca Naylor

Rebecca
Happy, fast, excited, nice
Brother and sister of Sam and Anna
Enjoys my hamsters, video games, and my family
Who feels excited when I go home, drawing, and happy with everybody I know
Who needs food when she's hungry, walks around to the store
With her sister or family, needs a hug when she's sad
Who gives hugs to her family, love to her family, who gives her hamsters food
Who fears fires, ghosts, floods
Who would like to dance, sing, and swim
Resident of Pennsylvania
Naylor

Just Remember Me
by Samantha Bonus

I hope to see you again, after my life is ruined
When I walk up to that door, as proud as I can be
I'll remember you
You're the only one who's stayed behind me in my need
You're my best friend in the world–get me
Yes you do!
I wish l were you, the way you handle things
I hate it when you're picked on, that really ticks me off
Just say hello, I'll be fine, I'll just be behind
I know that I'll be there whenever you're hurt
Just remember me, I'll be fine, just behind
Remember me, I'll be fine
Just say hello!
I'll just be behind, just remember me!

Emma
by Emma Campbell

Emma
Short, funny, animal lover and shy
Sister of Aimee and Claire
Enjoys ice skating, Molly and family time
Who feels tired, loved and warm in her heart
Who needs stuffed animals, pets and family
Who gives gifts on birthdays, help to Mom, and candy
Who fears making a fool of herself, her cat when she is mad and getting in trouble
Who would like to meet the President, be the President and make a vote
Resident of Pennsylvania
Campbell

Where I'm From
by Eden Hemmingson

I am from wind whistling through the leafy green trees
From jumping higher and higher with my brother on the trampoline
From loping around three barrels in a shamrock pattern
On a black and brown quarter horse
From climbing a gigantic dirt mound
While the cool soil runs through my fingers and toes
I am from roasting marshmallows to a dark crisp
From making warm, chewy s'mores
From listening to music that my mom plays on her guitar around the campfire
From two little black dogs, one old and one young
I am from hearing the timer go off on the stove
From biting into a freshly made chocolate chip cookie
From blowing candles out on my birthday
And hearing the paper rip when I open my presents
From having chocolate cake and vanilla ice cream
From having my friends spend the night for a party
I am from building thin little forts out of sticks and mud
From a farm with one silo and three barns
I am from a family of four
A dad, Brian; a mom, Joy; me, Eden; and a goofy little brother, Cash

Boss Fight
by Christopher Lloyd

My mom is fighting a boss with two tails
I will be heartbroken if she fails
Spells like cure, water, and thundaga
Leveler, darkness, fire and blizzaga
She is still trying with all of her might
Just keep on going and finish the fight
Come to my house and guess what you'll see?
Mommy and Daddy are gamers, just like me
Xbox 360, Playstation and Wii
All hooked up to the HDTV

Otters
by Aubrie Morley

Brown, fun
Swimming, paddling, splashing
Very talented swimming animals
Mammals

Grandpa, Come Home
by Peggy Sue Reynolds

Grandpa, why did you have to go?
Grandpa, I didn't even know
Grandpa, you left me all alone
Grandpa, come home
I went to your house one day
And guess what Grandma had to say?
"Grandpa isn't coming back"
Grandma said, "Dear, don't be sad,
I know you miss him really bad,
But he's in a better place
And we'll be there some day"
Grandpa, why did you have to go?
Grandpa, I didn't even know
Grandpa, you left me all alone
Grandpa, come home

Faces of Freedom
by Kate Kirkebak

The faces of freedom are like bells of beauty
Everyone hear them ring!
When people hear them
They come to hear the bells of beauty
Liberty the beauty
Liberty the great
Makes people feel safe as they enter our state
Immigrants can come and feel free
Freedom is beauty to all
And freedom is different to all
So I hope freedom will come
To all around the world

Dream Land
by Ashton Liston

Where the sound of waves fills my ears
Where I can bury my feet in the soft, warm sand
Reclining under the palm trees, as the hot sun beats down on the golden sand
Where flowers reach out, as if they're lending a helping hand
Where I can run, no destination, just running, as if I'm the only one here
So if you find this special place, and come in search of me
I'll be walking dimly, like a ghost
On the shores of my Dream Land

Reese
by Reese Robinson

Reese
Creative, energetic, hungry, lazy
Brother of Remlee
Enjoys playing Nintendo DS, watching TV, and playing with friends
Who feels relaxed every evening, happy when playing, and excited at Christmas
Who needs some time to relax when tired
Plays Pokemon when bored, and needs rest when sleepy
Who gives hugs to his mom, information to people who are stuck on their DS
And help with the Pokemon card game
Who fears deadly poison, the king cobra, and deadly spiders
Who would like to meet my cousins, go to a party and relax
Resident of Pennsylvania
Robinson

Garrett
by Garrett Mallory

Garrett
Happy, energetic, excited, jumpy
Brother of Ian
Enjoys Wii, tackling blankets
And eating Popsicles when my parents are not looking
Who feels hyper at Christmas, awake at night
And jumpy when playing Wii
Who needs Gatorade when he's thirsty, nightlights when he's scared
And a shower when he's stinky
Who gives kisses to his mom, encouragement to friends
And gives toys for Christmas
Who fears the dark, Scene It, and the toilet
Who would like to play Wii all day, make a giant fort, and get a puppy
Resident of Pennsylvania
Mallory

Where I'm From
by Rebekah Turnbull

I am from a big family, a family of seven. Chaos
Mushy and sloppy kisses at family get-togethers, far away family
I am from babysitting cousins and siblings
Staying at Grandma's house in the summer
Playing tricks on my grandma and having her play tricks on me
I am from being a Nebraska fan
Being a half Nebraskan and half South Dakotan
I am from living on small isolated farms
Living in small, peaceful towns; all around, dirt roads and tons of snow
Numb fingers, collecting eggs, hearing the cluck-cluck of the chickens
Lifting a heavy two buckets of water in the winter
Going ice skating on the frozen driveway
I am from school and gossip; from boring, confusing math
Books, AR points, and reading
English, spelling, science, art, PE, music
From writing poems like this one
The thrill of the last day of school
Wading in the creek, listening to arguing from my brothers

A Reason Not To Go Out In the Rain
by Carson Hofer

Don't go out in the rain
Without a coat
So you don't
Catch a cold
And be told
Again by a
Friend to try
Staying dry
In the rain

When I Look Out the Window
by Janell Burkett

When I look out the window I see anything
From turtles to bugs, anything
Close your eyes and think about what you have
Now that you think about it, you have it pretty good
Compared to others or classmates
When you look out the window
You see anything you want to see, it is your world
Think next time you look out the window
Look at the world around you, what do you think?
Listen to the sounds around you, just listen
Think, dream, when you look around the window

The Yellow Day
by Haley Tuller

As yellow as the sun, a little flower sits
Just as a bumble bee lands in the sand
With the wind you can see the leaves swaying in the breeze
When I chew my gum I feel very happy
I use my crayon to draw a school bus
As I pick up my cup and drink my lemonade
I watch the sun start to set
Just as I go to get my tent
I set it up and lay down on my blanket
With the stars towering above me, my day ends

I'm Sorry
by Randi Wiland

I'm sorry I pulled the cat's tail
I'm sorry I spilled my ginger ale
But it was so funny; you see, I laughed too hard
Juice flew out of my nose
Nobody knows where it goes
I'm sorry I laughed at you
But I wore your curlers, too
Your dress is a mess
You're depressed
I'm sorry I laughed at you!

Zyla
by Zyla Volkman

Zyla
Happy, artistic, smart, nice
Sister of Destiny, Sara, Jessica, Drummer
Enjoys checkers, doing my bed, and playing with my dog
Who feels happy playing with my dog, lonely with I'm alone
Hungry when it's lunch time
Who needs food, water, and a bed
Who gives help, love, and money
Who fears fires, snakes, and heights
Who would like to go to Waldameer, eat ice cream, and eat donuts
Resident of Pennsylvania
Volkman

If You Had a Pickle
by Corey Krepps

If you had a pickle
You could trade it in for a nickel
Or you could use it for a tickler
Or if you're fickle
You could keep your pickle

Gym
by Avery Boea-Gisler

Gym is fun
The gym is the place to workout
The gym totally rocks!
The gym is a good place to be
The gym has balls

Faces of Freedom
by Elizabeth Petersen

You
Are you a face of freedom?
The bellows you think, "Am I?"
And it comes to you
Nobody replaces our faces
They're always there
But maybe if we make a difference, we are too
The sky
It turns blue
Because you made a difference
The small things count
You helped us become free!

Kites
by Kaylie Ansell

Kites high in the sky
I wish I could fly
Just as high
In the sky
Up, up, up and away
It goes up in the sky
Oh, how I wish I could fly
That high
Now it's time to go
The kite is getting low
Oh no, the kite is getting low, oh! No!
Now I must go

Water
by Brittaney Richards

Water
Pure, clear
Flowing, dripping, running
Dancing in the river
Liquid

School
by Chase McCartney

I like it
Except for the learning
When I learned
My brain was burning

Animals
by Taren Gingerich

Animals in the forest
Live all around
Some live in trees
Some in the ground
Some are afraid
They run away
But some aren't
They just stay

The Thing
by Billy Cowell

Under the ground
By the pipe
Within the sewer
It flew up
Until it was
Among the stars
Is where it went

Bat
by Tre Brooks

Bats, bats, bats
Black
Bats, bats, bats
Vampire bats
Bats, bats, bats
Brown
Bats, bats, bats

The Invincible Ironman
by Joe LaRocca

Ironman the iron knight
He can really metal fight
He has pulsar beams
Ironman fulfilled his dreams

Cow
by Rachel Czulewicz

I know a cow named Moo-Moo
He always seemed so blue-hoo
He had a sad face
He walked a slow pace
And he likes to drink Yoo-Hoos

The Ocean
by Christina Kuerner

I like the ocean
The waves' quick motion
Showering right over me
How it is swell
Sitting by a shell
Listening to the sea
I like to swim
When the sky grows dim
Watching the creatures I see

Parakeets
by Huey Gillispie

Parakeets are very colorful
They are so wonderful
Parakeets like to sing
They also like to swing
Parakeets like food
After they have food they're in a good mood

In the Tree
by Faye Maccaglia

Look at me
In the maple tree!
Here comes the sap
I lick it up like that
It was not my base
Why was I there in the first place?

A Missing Bunny
by Anna Swink

The Easter Bunny missing …
Whatever will we do?
We looked in a store
And at the zoo
We looked in his kitchen
Oh, where are you?
The children are crying
The parents are whining
Oh Easter Bunny, we need you
We looked in the forest
And we looked at the park
We even looked at the mini mart
The only evidence we found
Were Easter eggs all over the ground!
We looked one more place
It was the candy store
We found the Easter Bunny filling up more
He said, "Oh dear, children
I lost track of time
I thought it was still quarter till nine!"

School
by Luke Desmond

School
Stressing, hard
Writing, working, thinking
Pennsylvania, Joe Walker, farm, trailer
Snoring, sleeping, eating
Relaxing
Home

Couplets
by Samantha Weiss

Little cousins love to play
They always get their way
When they win they say, "Yay!"
They watch the horses say, "Neigh!"
They watch the starry night
Little cousins make my sunny day!

Randall Jacobs
by Jacob Miller

People poetry
Randall Jacobs
Helpful, friendly
Nicely understandable
He is a good friend
If only I could be him

Untitled
by Hunter Sperling

Cactus
Soaking up heat
Tall as a building, long
Arms that stretch out, lives very long
Prickly

Old Man and His Car
by Rebecca Shuman

Do you hear that?
Oh, look
It's old man Bob
In his new car
I hear the horn
Honk, honk
Beep, beep
Toot, toot
Honk, honk
Beep, beep
Toot, toot
Do you hear, it is noisy
He screams, "Hey, what's new?"
Did you hear him?
"Nothing much, you?"
Light's flashing
Blink, blink
His lights are flashing, see?
He beeps his horn again
Do you hear that?

Bob
by Zachary Stimeling

Bob was on the green plants
Bob then jumped and lost his pants
Bob then got the cramps

Dog
by Courtney Hixenbaugh

Fluffy and furry
Playful and like to bury
Hearts go pumpy
They go jumpy
Leave in a big hurry
To watch squirrels scurry

Puppies
by Allison Lindley

Puppies
Fun to play with
Never ending playtime
Cute and caring
The trick masters
Best friends

Claire the Bear
by Cody Longstreth

Once there was a bear
Her name was Claire
She won a chair
At the fair
She ate a pear
And lost her hair
Now she was bare
But she didn't care

Trains
by Samantha Moore

Trains going from land to sea
Racing faster than the eye can see
Against the wind, snow, sleet, and hail
In and out of tunnels they go
Needing passengers for the ride
Stations keep passing by

Joe, My Brother
by Robin Thomas

Smart, calm
Sleeping, studying, listening
Helps me with my mistakes
Walking dictionary

A Little Rascal
by Maura Herbick

My pup is such a little rascal
He is such a ball of fun
Every day and every night
He shakes his little bum
My pup is such a little rascal
He always does something bad
I love him so and so
Even if he gets me mad
My pup is such a little rascal
His favorite thing to do is play
He was the funniest and the cutest
When we got him in May
My pup is such a little rascal
But he always has a smile
My pup is such a little rascal
Every once in a while

The Flag
by Jimmy Houser

Red is for the blood of the soldiers that have passed
White is for the peace we cannot have
Blue is for the sea that parts us now
With the red of the blood, the white of the peace
And the blue of the sea, the flag is born

Spring Is Here
by Tehya Brooks

Flowers start to bloom
The grass starts to turn green now
Gardens make more food

Being Grown
by Joi Sumler

You think you can do this, and that
But you're not grown
See, you think you're a big shot and you will never be stopped
But what you don't know is that there's always somebody to step on your toes
Before you know it, you're down in the blue
Without a clue because you thought you were grown
When you're down in the blue without a clue
Because you thought you were grown, you wonder, why?
Why didn't you listen
And why didn't you pay attention to the people who loved you?
Now you're down in the blue without a clue
Because you thought you were grown

The Moon
by Austin Mattocks

The moon is graceful
As the wolves cry beneath it
Moon goes when sun comes

Snow
by Amber Carbaugh

Snow is a beautiful, gentle blanket spreading over the ground
With its white beauty and pure heart blowing
Left to right snow is falling
Calling to the animals to come out and play the Eskimo way
Snowflakes falling down on me
Their gentle touch is wet and cold, mighty and bold
While falling to the ground, the mighty whiteness surrounds me
From head to toe, the snow seems to grow and grow
It continues to blow to the ground
Then there is no sound
Only darkness all around
It was night and now all the creatures were safe and sound

A Fun Way To Exercise
by Pamela McAllister

I stretch and stretch
And find it fun to stretch
And try to reach the sun
I bend and bend to touch the floor
Until the muscles in my legs get sore

Courageous Mom!
by Emily Boyd

Crystal
Tan, soft
Loving, caring, active
Her energy is for everyone
Mom

The Fox
by Sydney Powell

There is a fox at Uphill Lane
Who stares and smiles at me
He goes out in summer, spring, or rain
At first I thought he was a she
He is a running rain cloud above the city
Or like a speedy truck
He is like a top dog fox
One time he brought for me, a duck
The time he howled, it was like the roaring ocean calling to me
Or also like the mountains singing!
He runs as fast as a bumble bee
He loves the Old Town Clock's ringing
I will soon give him a name of his own
He is very fast and great
Last time I saw him, I knew that he had grown!
He has never ever been late
I love that fox
And he is almost all, all mine
I would even say he totally rocks!
I think that I will call him Brett!

Football
by Devin Holt

Football is an athletic sport
It keeps your blood running
Don't play football on a court
Or you won't look stunning
Don't shout to the floor
Just do your chore
Sometimes players weigh a ton
But playing football is still fun
A play can be called "Cover Three"
Just do your thing, don't hit a tree
Football, football is my game
Football is my middle name

My Pap
by Bailey Anderson

Pap
Nice, skinny
Buying, selling, giving
Died on Christmas Day
Grandpa

The Bat and Cat
by Ala Small

There once was a bat
Her name was Pat
She was not very fat
She was friends with a cat
His name was Matt
Pat was glad that Matt didn't like cats
They both liked to wear hats
One day Pat sat on a rat
Then the rat was flat
So Matt ate the flat rat

My Cat and Dog
by Kimberly Belisky

My cat is fat
His name is Flap
He sleeps on a mat
Flap loves to nap
Flap hates my dog, Gat
When she pats and disturbs his nap
Then I have to pat
So I get their attention with a clap
That makes Flap go to his mat
And Gat just sits on my lap
A few minutes later, where is Gat?
Then I look, she's sleeping with Flap
Flap is finally friends with Gat
And Gat is finally friends with Flap

Spring Is Coming
by Jayden Cools

Winter has gone home
Bright green grass, daisies turn bright
That tells spring is here

Dogs
by Joey Carney

Dogs are so cute
They chew on your boot
My dog went missing
So I was listening
And he came back and went to mute

Ice Cream
by Kristen Luzell

I love ice cream, it's so good
So great that you won't want to wait
So try it please, if you don't I'll be sad
And you might even go mad
You need it to live, I think
So don't you dare blink
Oh, whoops, wrong story I'm telling
So start selling
Of the ice cream of course!
Everyone needs some, old and young
You also have to be nice to your tongue!
So thanks for reading
And I hope you have some ice cream today

Winter
by Melissa Boob

Frigid snowflakes
Falling all over town
Friendly snowmen
Standing outside my window
Frosty snow cones
Melting near the fire
Chilly wind
Blowing through the trees
Soft puppies
Cuddling on my lap
Warm hot cocoa
Spilling in my mouth

Angels
by Madelynn Moyer

Her face was fair and rosy; her eyes spoke peace and love
From her back, fluffy feathers, wings as from a turtle dove!
As she sang, oh so sweetly, tiny stars fell from her flowing hair
Mermaids swim, the fairies dance
As they do that, the angels watch over us

The Ghosts of Halloween
by Madison Yarborough

The ghosts of Halloween
Are very scary sights
If you take one look at them
You'll be up all night
The ghosts of Halloween
Are mean and foul
And if you listen closely
You can even hear them growl

Love From the Heart
by Emma Ewing

The love that I feel is fabulous
The love that I see is like summer bliss
This love does not come around everyday
This love is awesome I must say
The love that I am talking about is warm and from the heart
This love reminds me of beautiful art
My family is how I define this word called love
My dad, my mom, and my sister to speak of

A Blue Day
by Zachary Etzel

I wake up and everything is blue
My mom is brewing up a stew
My dad is reading the news
I just got a bruise
By kicking a ball
Off the brick wall
No wonder everything is blue
Caden put goo in the glue!

The Hurricane Disaster
by Surabhi Beriwal

In the gigantic ocean
Where everything is warm
A storm is gaining power
A hurricane is starting to form
I hear a person cry
"A hurricane is near
You'll escape if you try
Or lose everything you have here"
The air is getting colder, the waves are getting faster
And the change of destruction is getting vaster
After hours of storms going on and on
The endless pain is finally gone

B.F.F.
by Caroline Raftis

Friends forever
Times together
We always have fun
In the bright sun
We like to run
In the sun
It is bright
We don't fight
Well, we might
Have a fight
But we'll get over it
And do a split
We have sleepovers
We're chocolate lovers
We share things
And we sing
We also dance
In pink pants
All day
Every day

Butterfly
by Tristan Gilligan

Flying all the way
Only in the day
Normally in May
Flies a butterfly
In the morning sky
Up, up, up so high

The Things of Nice and Mean
by Keegan Fischer

Nice
Friendly, fun
Sharing, caring, helping
Happy, funny, grouchy, sad
Happy, funny, grouchy, sad
Lying, sneaking, stealing
Selfish, boring
Mean

Spring
by Brittany Watts

Spring is such a wonderful time
I see the sun and have lots of fun
Take a splash in the pool
Have a drink of lemonade … cool
Don't worry, there's enough for everyone!
So come with us and have some fun
Experience spring!

Detention
by Allison Reams

Kids drooling
In boring detention
It's because
No one's paying attention
In classes

My Terrific Mom
by Brandie Hartwiger

My mom is really special, she is really nice to me
She helps me with my problems, and is as polite as can be
When my mom tells me about her day, some things are really funny
When I do something for her, she says it makes her day sunny
She knows that she gets mad at me when I don't do something her way
I really hate to upset her, "So I'll do it," I always say
When I don't have a good day at school, she tells me everything will be okay
She'll try to cheer me up, so then we'll go out for a special day
When my mom has a short temper and gets upset, just like a mother
It doesn't matter much, because I'll always love her

My Mom
by Tara Shaffer

My mom is very sweet
She is so loving to me
She takes me to the park
But sometimes she is as busy as a bee
We walk around the block at night
I can't wait until I can be with her
When she comes home from work
We can chat with the neighbor
Sometimes she is nice
But at times gets mad during the day
When she yells
I feel like I want to run away
She bugs me at times
So I do my homework at night
She wants me to do my best
She smiles when I get everything right
My mom will get mad at me
Just like all mothers sometimes do
But that doesn't matter so much
'Cause I still love her
Love, Tara

The Beach
by Alexandra Wilson

The wind, the waves, the gentle breeze
The sand, the sound, the smell of seas
The shouting, and playing, waiting and waiting
To join the fun again

Leaves
by Kaila Glenn

Leaves all over the ground
Orange, green, yellow, and brown
Crunch, crunch under my feet

Basketball
by Lillian Riggleman

I am a basketball fanatic
I shoot, I score, and I am good at it
I can pump-fake and go to the hoop
Heck yeah, I can scoop
I can go to the baseline and shoot a reverse lay-up
If you're betting on someone else, then go ahead, pay up
I am better than you, don't you see?
Are you sure you want to go one-on-one with me?

The Man Who Was Late
by Gianna Leone

There once was a man who was late
Just because of a plate
But you don't have to worry
Because he was in a hurry
To meet a woman named Kate

Spring's Arrival
by Jenny Byham

As I get out of bed, not everything's the same
When I look out my window, I notice the birds that came
They're singing their songs as spring is coming
I rush out to play, skipping and humming
As I see all the blooms, I just can't believe it
I look all around and try to receive it
I get on my bike and ride around
I think that spring has finally been found

Our Future
by Michael Mickey

A poem of our future is what I'll write
If we make these changes soon, our kid's future maybe bright
As we sit here and look away
Thousands of trees are cut down each day
Drinkable water we send to the drain
Yet thousands of people suffer thirsty pain
And burn up oil like we are going insane
We need to stop doing the things we do
For if we do not, there will be no future for me or for you

Sounds
by Lindsey Bilski

Sounds can travel everywhere
Sounds can travel in the air
Sounds can travel in big waves
Sounds echo off of walls in caves
Bouncing at a very high speed
Fast as lightning takes the lead
I still have wonders in my head
Pulling me to my last thread
I love sound waves!

War
by Johnathan Mazur

I like to play my game
One day it will lead me to fame
I'll fight battles till the end
The evil enemy is not my friend

All the Clouds
by Dominique Gross

Sun
Bright, yellow
Floats, heats, warms
The sun feels good
Star

Spring Is Beautiful
by Justine Tucker

Easter and daisies
Kites and airplanes in blue skies
Rainbows and roses

Haunted
by Corrine Silvio

Scary
Ghosts whispering
Footsteps heard everywhere
Tourists heard something here
Ghosts!

A Beautiful Flower
by Brittney Fitschen

I see a pretty
Flower, so bright and light, so
Beautiful and nice

Aliens
by Courtney Punchur

Scary
Ooey, gooey
Inkie, dinkie, pinkie
The aliens are scary

Acorns
by Rimee Porter

Acorns, acorns
Everywhere
All over the ground
And in my hair
I tried to get them out
With a glare
But they just dance around
In my hair

PennDOT/Daddy
by P. J. Mitten

Father
Works hard
Has big truck
Gets serious about sports
Harry

Boys
by Charlee Kimmel

Weird
Flinging erasers
Made in China
They are made odd
Scary

Butterfly
by Marley Corkle

Butterfly flutter
Butterfly fly
Butterfly twinkle
High in the sky

My Haiku
by Isabella Gilbert

Five syllables here
Over here are seven more
Are you happy now?

Remix of Pants
by Katelyn Smith

I know a lot of people who wear pants
One of them is my pastor, Tim Dance
Yes, at church he works a lot
Almost like a story with a plot

Basketball
by Hannah Gayle

I love to play basketball
On a really big court
In the middle of winter
Because it's a really fun sport

Soccer
by Emily Ziegelmeier

Soccer is fun
You get to play
You kick and push
That's the way!

My Fish
by Laura Savin

My fish is slow
It will swim below
The water line
I can't see its outline
It died late last night
When I turned out my light
I buried it under my bed
But he said ...
You are mean
You have to clean
Since there is trash
I will crash

Grasshoppers
by John Peterson

Grasshoppers live, eat
Bees and wasps are evil stings
Grasshoppers be safe

The People At School Are the Best
by Kaitlin Hudak

The people at school are the best
They are loving and kind
They make me feel so blessed
They're like a wonderful find
The teachers want us to grow
They try to make us smart
They give us facts to know
They teach with all of their heart
The students are always quite happy
They like to be joking and funning
Our uniforms look quite snappy
Our smiles make the room sunny
We all get along like buddies
Yet it causes us much frustration
That we toil all day at our studies
While we long for our summer vacation

Faces of Freedom
by Rylee Homandberg

Flying free like an eagle
I will never let go
It makes my life full
So good to be home
Lady Liberty welcomes you
So still she will be
From the top of the mountains
To the deep of the sea
Our leaders have led them
Free we may be
The faces of freedom
That occur to me

Screech Owl
by Collin Rothfuss

Screech owl
Big, silent
Zipping, zooming, hunting
Has different phases of color
Bird

Under the Sea
by Andrew Johnson

In my submarine I look out of my window
I see fish of all different kinds in large groups
The bubbles the fish breathe look like bubble gum bubbles
The teeth of the sharks look like knives from the kitchen
During my discovery I have seen lots of stuff
Some facts I have shared and some I have not
Now it is time to go out and look for more!

Honey and Crackers
by Evan Pugh

Honey and crackers, in the night
Honey and crackers, out of sight
Honey and crackers, to the bite
Honey and crackers, are just right

I Love My Mom
by Laken Brandt

I love you and you love me
And that's the way it should always be
No matter what I say or what I do
I'll always be a part of you

Baseball
by Hank Shultz

Baseball is good
Baseball is bad
It can be both!
Baseball can be the mound and home runs!
Baseball can be fun!
Baseball can be dumb!
Baseball is ...
Candy
Worms
Flies
Wings
Webs

Why Am I So Unlucky?
by Carley Blanchard

I don't know why I'm so unlucky
Maybe it's because I'm really mucky
Why am I so unlucky?
Is it because of my chicken cock-a-doodle-doo
Or my cow named Moo?
Why am I so unlucky?
I never win or wash the dirty clothes bin
Why am I so unlucky?
I never go on missions or believe in superstitions
I'm so unlucky

Autumn
by Lydia Kirkpatrick

As the leaves fall
I go outside and have a ball!
I rake and rake all day
Once I'm done I get to play!
I jump and roll in the leaves on the ground
My laughter is the only sound!

Violets Are Violets
by Tori Austin

Violets are violet, not blue
Roses are red
But none of
These flowers are as I love you
Trees are green
Clouds are white
Trees tower boldly overhead
Yet clouds are soft, fluffy, and light

Dinosaurs
by Josiah Wilson

Dinosaurs are strong and very mighty!
Thunder and lighting are also!
I like them a lot!
I like them, do you?

All Dinosaurs
by Ryan Snell

For all the dinosaurs that make you frown
All of them maybe walked through town
The Tyrannosaurus, he loved to eat the Lambeosaurus
Another dinosaur is the Coelophysis, he certainly is not the nicest!
The last dinosaur is the Velociraptor, he can't get away without laughter

The Hiking Leprechaun
by Devin Morton

The leprechaun is riding a bike
Because he is on a hike
He moved far away
To a big stack of hay
He lives with his nice cousin Mike

Air
by Nikol Siple

Air, I need you to share
Air, I need a pear
Air, I don't need a bear
Air, I need you to share
Your air with me!

Dog
by James Duchi

The dog was so tired
He couldn't work so he got fired
He went to play in the barn
He found a ball of yarn
He played with it all day
Finally he lost it in the hay

Striped Owl
by Tianni Reibsome

Saw-whet Owl
Small, quick
Hunting, swooping, calling
They blend in with the trees
Birds

Books
by Savannah Harden

Books, books, books
Sad books, happy books
Thin, fat, long books
Old, new, short books
Those are just a few
Weird books, joke books
Calming, frustrating, loving books
Joking, informational, entertaining books
Sports books, too
Interesting books, boring books
Funny books, don't forget crazy books
Last of all–best of all–
I like friendship books

Elf Owl
by Emily Hemphill

Elf owl
Tiny, brown-gray
Hunting, catching, eating
When captured, it fakes death
A desert bird

Friend
by Caitlin Zeher

A friend is nice
A friend is someone who lends you rice
A friend is someone you can always trust
When you need some help in the dust
You can catch a friend in a run
Or you'll catch a friend in the sun
You'll see a friend out and about
But you won't see them in a pout
A friend stands up for you
And they don't say boo
There comes a friend to help you guide
And be on your side
Here comes my friend now

Silly
by Gabriella Zarragoitia

There's a silly, willy, illy girl
Who lives in the clouds, above the sea shore
She laughs all night, she laughs all day
And makes jokes beyond the Milky Way
The clouds laugh along and say
"We'll laugh at your jokes, even through May"
That night the girl was quieter than she'd ever been
The clouds woke up the next morning
And she was gone in the wind

Marc-André Fleury
by Zachary Maxwell

There once was a goalie named Fleury
He always had to hurry
He was so fast
But not too fat
But his helmet was so blurry

Jasper
by Natasha Gareis

Jasper is cuddly
Jasper is fluffy
Jasper is pretty
Jasper is my puppy
I love him
He loves me
He is my best friend
Together we make a great team

Great Grey Owl
by Zachary Smith

Owl
Fearless, fierce
Nesting, sneaking, swooping
The biggest type of owl
Great Grey

Big Brother Jason
by Morgan Williams

Big brother Jason
Runs over to his little sister
To ask her to race
Even though she does not want to
She still races with her brother

The Old Pete
by Rhig Lacey

I once owned a truck
It was a '64 Pete
It wasn't very sweet
It was tough
Most people say, "Yuck!"
'Cause it's dirty and oily
The electricity cords are coily
The interior is full of rust and stuff
The lights are dull
The tires are dirty
The frame is sturdy
And the engine is grimy

Graveyard
by Bobbi Jo DeVor

The graveyard–a place to let out things you've done
Without hurting someone you love or to visit someone who died
Possibly someone very close to you
You would do anything to bring them back
But as much as you want to cry, you won't
Because you know they would want me to be happy–
As you stand above their grave you can feel them watching you
And wishing they could see you one more time
And say I love you and never let go
But they must, just the thought of it makes you cry
You start to think of all the things you didn't have the chance to say
And all the things to say sorry for
You think to yourself (I've lost my chance)
As you stand above their grave, the crying stops
You start to feel your loved ones with you
It comforts you
The crying starts again, this time tears of joy
You know they forgive you–
As you step off their grave you start to forgive yourself–
As you remember all the memories of your loved ones

Bella
by Connor Lindsay

My dog named Bella
She catches snowballs in the air
But does not catch sticks
She makes me laugh when she licks me
My loving dog named Bella

Snowy Owl
by John Paul Uzialko

Snowy owl
Silent, protective
Swooping, resting, calling
It is camouflaged
Bird

School
by Shania Vincent

I have to go to school
That is not cool
I do not like it
I'd rather sit in a basket
At least it has a pool

Tiger
by Maura Ward

Tiger
Bold, sharp
Pouncing, sleeping, jungle
Loud, big, soft, quiet
Swimming, resting, graceful
White, orange
Swan

The Ocean
by Brianna Jones

The ocean smoothly passed by me
It softly crashed on the shore
It made the boats bobble up and down
It calmly splashed my face
It glistened in the sun
It is full of fish
The ocean is full of dolphins
It is full of trigger fish, starfish, and turtles
It makes me feel as if I just flew up in the sky
And I'm resting on a cloud
As I go under, the tiny bubbles float from my mouth

That Special Dream Girl
by Joseph Serafini

I once had a dream about a girl
Who really gave me a whirl
She was blonde with blue eyes
She could not say good-bye
She was as pretty as a pearl
I really liked her so
She said, "I like you, Joe
You're my best beau
I'm glad you know that I don't want to go"
I woke up from the dream
I was real mad at me
'Cause I thought it was real
But I had to deal
So I couldn't really scream
I was sad at the beginning
But it was the bottom of the inning
The girl was not there
I'm serious, I swear
So I'm not really grinning

Snowflakes
by Maysun Savelli

My snowflake is called
Valentine Snowflake
It tastes like love
It feels like a heart
Sounds like a heart thumping
It smells like a heart
That is how I describe my snowflake

Advent/Christmas
by Davis Nemmers

Advent
Pink, purple
Praying, waiting, preparing
Patience, life, tree, Jesus
Singing, dancing, rejoicing
Joyous, happy
Christmas

Guardian Angel
by Bethany Bauer

My guardian angel with wings so white
She watches over me both day and night
She comforts me with her love so rare
But in my heart I know she's there
Through rain, sleet, and snow
I know she'll get me where I need to go
I would have loved to have met her
But I know she'll be in my heart forever

What Will Happen To Us All
by Emily Leister

Weathering, erosion
Even trash in the sea
Humans are polluters
As far as I can see
Ice melting
Where the penguins slide
Weathering where
The poor animals hide
People are disgraceful
And so am I
Because in the future
Everything will die
No more people
No more things
Only a ground
And wind that can't sing
Shriveled up plants
And dried up waters
No more fabrics for pants
No more colder or hotter

Dreams
by Natalia Conte

Sometimes I lay awake in my bed wondering ...
What will become of me one day?
Will I be the girl that every neighbor envies
Or a girl who envies everyone?
Will I be the picture of success
Or barely have food on the table?
I trust what God has in store for me
So from now on all I can do is dream
My heart tells me to not worry
But my mind says think
I know that the only way my dreams will ever come true
Is to wish, dream, and make them reality

I Feel Precious
by Brianna Donoghue

I feel precious like a butterfly
Flying free in the rain forest
I feel like the sun in the sky
Lighting the whole Earth
Precious like a rainbow on a sunny day
With raindrops tapping on roof tops
(tap, tap, tap)
I feel precious

Depression
by Tommie Elias

Depression is black like a big tar road
Depression is spiky like a porcupine
It smells like sweat
Depression sounds like hissing cockroaches
Depression feels like dry dirt
It makes me feel down

Anger
by Joshua Coleman

Anger is black like a never-ending pit
Anger is cold like the coldest winter
It smells like burnt rubber
It tastes like burnt chicken
It sounds like an angry bear
It has a texture like the scales on a snake
It moves like a lion stalking its prey
Anger makes me feel crazy

Over the World
by Nathan Law

Over the world I see ships and planes
All over the world from the ground to the sky
In my tiny spaceship, I see lots of things
I see the moon, the sun, and our little world
All over the world I see ships and planes
All over the world from the ground to the sea

Kangaroo
by Brandon Kent

I, I, a choo
I see a kangaroo
I like to sleigh
We do it all day
My cat likes Lou

Outside
by Jackie Foran

There outside, what's out there?
Leaves flying to the ground everywhere
A peaceful place, where birds nest
Sunlit grass, moonlight crest
Through the seasons, I watch the world change
Summer, winter, fall, spring, as I watch my open range
I'm lonely as I watch aside
Now I think I'll go outside

The Villain
by Carly Williams

One day there was a girl named Paige
Then a villain stuck her in a cage
She felt so very sad
But at the same time she was mad
But for the rest of her life there she lay

Mason
by Jakob Richardson

Mason is a monkey
He was so junky
He met a woman
That had some pudd'n
He is so funky

Megan
by Hayley Patchen

I have a friend named Megan
One day I might go to her house again
We are friends
I hope our friendship never ends
I like Megan

Old Man
by Paige Brumett

There was an old man from the moon
Everyone thought he was a loon
Because he ate birds
But then he soon learns
That he should return home soon

The Cat and the Bat
by Jessica James

There once was a cat
Who tried to eat a bat
But the bat got her
And took out all her fur
Then the cat went kersplat

The Dog Who Wanted To Be a Stunt Dummy
by Collen Hornaman

There once was a dog who lived in a bog
He kept a nice blog
He wanted to be
A stunt dummy
Then he found a big, fat log

Elf Owl
by Ian Lininger

Elf owl
Small, short
Soaring, gliding, hunting
Lives in dry lands
Hunter

The Big Man
by Nicole Blauser

There was a man
He loved to can
He was very fat
And had a large cat
Then for the rest of his life he had a big fan

The Bee's Tree
by Joshua Burgess

I climbed up a tree
I saw a little bee
I gave it a pie
It started to die
Then I got stung by the bees

The Dog
by Chris Nichols

There was a dog
Who loves to run in the fog
Who loves pie
Who loves to lie
Who was a hog

The Shark's Great Bite
by Charles Culver

There was a shark
His name was Bark
He had a great bite
That can go right through a tight armor knight
And that is the story of Bark

Flowers
by Julia Brooks

Flowers, flowers, flowers
Pretty flowers, cut flowers
Dry, dead, forgotten flowers
Alive, beautiful, hope-giving flowers
Those are just a few
Wet flowers, planted flowers
Blooming, living, flowing flowers
Growing, budding, beginning flowers
Colorful flowers, too
Pink flowers, violet flowers
Wonderful flowers, don't forget plastic flowers
Last of all–best of all–
I like the flowers I grow!

Up the Stairs
by Levi Day

When I go up the stairs without the lights
My fears come out and have a fight
Right beside me is a light at my fears
Then I see out of their eyes teeny, tiny tears
Then they vanish into thin air

Lilies
by Therese Jaglowski

Lilies, beautiful
Lilies, white as snow
Lilies are lovely

Flowers
by Ara Shwani

Flowers, flowers, flowers anywhere
There are roses, daisies, bluebells, and even more
Flowers are a part of nature
Flowers bloom and blossom when they're ready
When you see flowers, remember this poem
Flowers!

Birds and Freedom
by Cody Davis

I am a bird lover
They are really sweet
They fly so high
And sing tweet, tweet
I admire their freedom
Because we are all the same
The bald eagle represents our country
That is strong, not lame
I love my country, America
Our soldiers are so brave
Let the birds bring them home
For another life, and our freedom they can save

Jonas Brothers
by Lauren Brosko

There are these three boys
You can say they amaze me
They can sing, act, and are so perfect
It is just plain crazy!
The guys I am thinking of
Are Nick, Joe, and Kevin
They are like heroes
You could say they're angels from Heaven
These brothers are so talented
It's illogically true
I listen to their music
Day and night through
I think of them all the time
Even in my dreams
I love them so much
Even more than it seems
I'd do anything to meet them
It would be the greatest day ever
That would be one memory
I would cherish forever!

Yellow
by Rachel Moore

Yellow is ...
Fluffy as a feather
Sour as a lemon
Bright as the sun
Lovely as a flower
Soft as a pillow
Shaped like a noodle
A sound like ocean waves
Feels like silk
Tastes sweet, like lemonade
Makes me feel happy and excited
Cute as a newborn baby
Trustworthy like a friend
Loving like a puppy

Emma
by Emma Saftner

Short, strong, diligent, friendly
Daughter of Heather and Clay
Lover of gymnastics, presents, and ranch pretzels
Who feels excited on two hour delays, tired when woken up too early
And happy to go to church on Sundays
Who finds happiness in going to the beach, hugs, and friends
Who needs comfort in the dark, to do art with Makenzie, and a good stain stick
Who gives attention to younger children, and gently used toys to the needy
Who fears being alone and the unknown
Who would like to see Heaven, Shawn Johnson in person
And my family win a trip to Hawaii
Who enjoys swimming, country music, and watching "The Lord of the Dance"
Who likes to wear cropped tights, leotards, and plaid skirts
Resident of Pennsylvania

Dear Dad
by Roisin Sabol

Dear Dad
I love you
And Mom, too
But I don't know what to do
I am bored
I already sold my hoard
Of brown ink pens
And my three pet hens!
Can we please go somewhere?
C'mon, we'll be out of Mom's hair!
How about the mall
Or Town Hall?
Or maybe
We could visit Erica's baby!
There's a lot that we could do
But we won't make a fuss
How about we take the bus?
Dead Dad
Thank you very much
From your ten year old honey bunch!

St. Anselm
by Jessica Bair

Word of God, that's my school
My name is Jessie and I am cool
Yeah, fifth grade, here to represent
Always Catholic from Christmas to Lent
Holy Water, use it every day
It's my secret weapon to keep Satan away
Hail to Mary, she's the one
Who gave birth to the Son
He saved us all by His grace
One day we will see Him face to face
When we get to that better place

Softball
by Zackary Wise

Baseball
Running, throwing
Catching, hitting, practice
Friends, home runs, coach, hits
Softball

My Grandpa
by Kourtney Thomas

I remember one day when I was small
I always asked Grandpa to play ball
Spending time with Grandpa made me happy
He always said, "Yes, now let's be snappy"
We played and played in the hot sun
Time would fly when we were having fun
He would say, "Go Kourtney, run fast"
Memories are like friendships, they last and last
He died one day and left me alone
I miss him even more now that I have grown
Grandpa never said any words of goodbye
Everyday that passes I always ask myself, "Why?"

Best Friends Forever
by Leah Deitt

Best friends are always there
And they always, always, always care
Best friends never talk about you behind your back
When you are around each other you both go wack
Best friends never lie
But they will surely help you get a guy
Best friends make you laugh when you feel sad
You do the same if they feel bad
Best friends call each other sisters
When a boy picks on you they say, "Don't you dare do that mister!"
Best friends sometimes fight
But that is what sisters do too, sometimes, right?
Most importantly, best friends stay together
Not just for a day or two, but forever

The Snow
by Katherine Dudt

I like the snow that comes in the winter
I like it when the sun comes out
The snow sparkles like a diamond
It's all very beautiful
I love the snow that stays on the trees
The trees that no longer have leaves or bees
I am so glad it is lovely
I am so glad God made it wonderfully
When the moon comes out
The snow is a group of stars
The star makes me a star too
It is like the universe
The world is like a big cake
And the snow is the sprinkles
Some children who play outside eat the snow
And inside is dirt and they do not know!
It gets very cold outside
And makes everything quiver
The wind goes by and makes me shiver
But, though it may be cold, it is very beautiful

Yellow
by Emma Orcutt

Ms. Liberty is green
Brown is the sand
Yellow is the sun
I catch in my hand
Green is my cottage
The lake is blue
Yellow is the butterfly
That lands on my shoe
Red is a rose
Peach is a child
Yellow is a daffodil
That grows in the wild

A Strong Snow
by Emily Critelli

Look at the snow
As it falls down
Like a piece of paper
Floating to the ground
Nice and slow
The way it trickles
But it gives you a feeling
A rather strong one
'Cause when it touches your eyelash
It sort of tickles!

I Wish I Could Fly
by Maria Esposito

I wish I could fly
High in the sky
To see the birds
Fly in herds

Summary
by Kara Pyo

A warm breeze in the air
A flower that blew in my hair
Palm trees sway
Oceans have waves
The sun so bright
When darkness comes there is no light
The sand is warm
There is no harm
In the summer

Homeland
by An Nguyen

My homeland is very far
When you look south east you see that shiny star
My homeland is Vietnam
It's not a free county
But it's my specialty
I speak it
I hear it
I read and I write it all the time
One dime here is $1,006 in Vietnam
It's a poor country
But I'm going to visit this year
Because my homeland is the land
I want to be near

I'm Away At School
by Jared Lombardi

Mom, I went to school
And I'm playing around
Listening and learning
Like I always do
Helping and talking
Like I always do
Have a great summer
And sweet dreams to you

My Undead Mummy and Me
by Nicholas Fegley

We walk to school everyday
We yell at the bullies
That get in our way
He's wrapped in bandages
We say he's the best mummy any day!

Sunshine
by Jacob Miaczynski

Sunshine, sunshine, so shiny and hot
Beautiful and yellow
It's a great camera shot!
Sunshine, sunshine
It's summer; I scream when it's summer
There is ice cream!
I want to have ice cream while
Watching a baseball team!
I love sunshine
I love it a lot!
But at the end of the day, the beautiful sunshine goes away!
Then I remembered what fun I had!
The ice cream scream, and having it at a baseball game!
The weather man says, "We will have much more sunshine tomorrow!"

The Evening and Night
by James Nassur

You are playing a video game
When in the room your mother came
She said, "It is time to go to sleep"
She does not want to hear a peep
When you are in your bed
You might feel very cozy
She says, "Goodnight Ted"
Then you say, "Goodnight Rosy"
You are having a dream
It is about a baseball team
If you want to be bright
Then go to bed at night

Dreams
by Christine McCullough

Without dreams I would only be
Very simply me
Dreams help us to come alive
On dreams we live and thrive
With dreams we can go anywhere
We can be a sailor, or have long black hair
We could travel on horseback across the plains
We can explore a cave as soon as it rains
We can hunt for lost or stolen treasure
We could find happiness beyond all measure
We can dream of being a monster or beast
We could even sit with our friends at a royal feast
In dreams we can rise to touch the sky
Or watch dogs playing while we fly by
We can sit and count the birds all day
Or write poems in every different way
But who would want to do that?

Cautious Mouse
by Mary Ann Markle

Creeping steadily
Watching its back for a cat
Hiding in corners

Blue Skies Ahead
by Rebecca Scassellati

Circling white clouds
Suddenly rip like cotton
Patch of blue shows through

Fight
by Matt Colosimo

Fight
Fisticuffs, fist fight, tussle
I have lots of muscle

Super
by Allison Singhose-Painter

Super, fabulous, glorious
Splendid, divine
You are so fine!

My Brother
by Zane Culp

His name is Kyle
He is so fat
He ran the mile
And looks like a cat
He is really funny
He is so rude
He has no money
But likes to eat food
He's afraid of the ghost
He gets really mad
He eats a lot of toast
And never becomes glad!

Fires
by Dustin Miller

Look, smoke floating out of a house; I see a fire!
Bright lights, flashing fast
Part of the roof is caving in!
Homeowners are standing, scared!
Now the homeowners are yelling
Here come more fire trucks, they stop
Pshhh, everybody hears the fire crackling
Boom! The wood beams just fell
The house looks wet and black
The fire fighters' equipment is pitch black
It smells like a campfire being put out
Homeowners are scavenging
The fire took a long time to put out
Trucks are leaving as the homeowners are devastated!

The Night Sky
by Leah Bross

The stars are bright
The moon is right
As they are up there in the bright night
As the airplanes fly through the night
Through the meadows and through valleys
The light comes from the night
As the airplanes crash down in the night
The stars are the brightest in the sky
It might make me cry
But the moon is still right in the dark, dark night
The stars are still the brightest in the little, little sky
The stars are just right

Painting
by Erin McNeal

As the paint dripped from the brush
Blip! Blip!
The paper became moist with watercolors
Puddles of colors would ruin the paper
So you would think ...
She slid the brush across the paper
As gentle as night falling
The streaks, lines, and shapes formed a picture
Though blabs and smudges spread on the page
Like butter on bread
She had completed something
No one else ever could

Denver
by Julie Harris

Denver is my dog
He loves to play
He likes to chase birds
He likes to lie in the creek
He is very friendly
He likes to jump on people

The Future I See
by Rieko Copeland

A boom, a bang
A crash in my ear
My eyes fill up with millions of tears
The sight I see
The war in Iraq
Soldiers fight for America
Though some never come back
We've tried to stop the war in Iraq
Though it's not very easy to bring them back
We are the future for our nations
We will stop the war for our generations
Though the fight will be long and hard
We will never, ever, drop our guard

Come To Me
by Richie Kopps

I think I'm moving now–and I have no fear
I try to keep moving, but it's way too far–
I've been moving from the start–these steps are not far apart
I wanna move back, it's just way too hard–these dreams are not takin' me nowhere–
Why'd I dream if they're not the truth–I wanna dream of something just like you–
Come to me–you see me movin', but you won't come here–
Why'd I look if you didn't care–come to me–it's a new life–and I know I'm scared–
Why'm I fallin' now–just no catch for me–come to me–
You see me movin', but you won't come here–why'd I look if you didn't care–
Think I'm movin', but go nowhere–pause and look around, tell me what you see–
This land is not made for me–
Come to me–come to me–come to me–just come to me–

Hard Work
by Kendra Zaruda

Planting and sowing
Is breaking my back
Oh and mowing
I work and I work
And it surprisingly
Does not pay off

Eve's Leaves
by Teagan Russ

Eve's leaves are the color of the moon at noon
Eve licked the spoon
She plays in the light of the moon
She nuzzles a small cocoon
She loves to run in the sun
And have fun

Flowers
by Amanda Hanan

I blossom in spring
And bloom in April
I am such a beautiful sight to see
I am a flower
Bees like to buzz around me, you see

My Friends
by Heather Serpico

I have many friends
I have hundreds of friends
I open them day and night
And fall in love with them
When I open them they speak their words
And lure me into a new world
In those worlds
I go on adventures and solve mysteries
In those worlds
I can do stuff that is real or make-believe
In those worlds
I feel so free I can do anything
If you wonder
Where in the world I got these wonderful friends
Well, you have them too
And they're standing right there upon your bookshelf
Begging you to open them

Friends
by Gavin Ennis

Friends are people full of love and care
Friends are the people who will always be there
Through times of distress, and times of despair
Friends will be there, ready to care
They help when you're in need
And care when you bleed
They're there by your side
To follow and guide
To help everyday
To lighten the way
Friends

Lamb
by Chase McKnight

A lamb is a lamb, hopefully it's not a ham
They are cute, fluffy, and white
They soar through the field like a kite
They are gentle and calm; they do not bite or put up a fight
They are not horses, donkeys, lions, or hippos
A lamb is a lamb, hopefully it's not a ham

Basketball
by Christina Didiano

Dribble, pass, shoot and score
They scored two and we scored four
All tied up with seconds to go
Can my teammate make the throw?
Hurry! Bring it up the court
The time is really running short
The buzzer sounds, it's overtime
They fouled me and I'm at the line
Focus, breathe, shoot, I'm fine
Swish! It's in!
Yes! We win

The Best Mom Ever
by Maria Rhine

My mom is really wonderful
My mom is the best
She helps me all the time
I am truly blessed
I can't wait to walk with her
Around our neighborhood and back
I also hope to go to Greensburg
To scrapbook and buy things on racks
My mom hates to do laundry
But with me she loves to relax and play
She takes me to my practices
But often she's busy and just can't stay
She is a great pharmacist
Separating all kinds of pills
She is really so kind
She even donates to the local Goodwill
There is no better mom in the world
This I know is true
I will always love her ... this is a fact
And she loves me through and through
Love,
Maria

Up To Bat
by Jared Jordan

Step up to the plate
Get ready to bat
Don't make a mistake
You'll hold the team back
He's eyeing up home
The wind-up, the pitch
It looks like a fastball
It made a big zip!
It's coming in fast
Keep your eye on the ball
The swing, a big crash
And guess what?
It's gone

Red Rose
by Anna Chensny

There lies a red rose, a child in a crimson cap
There lies a mystery waiting to be solved
And there lies an innocence about to be withered
Right there lies a red rose

The Rain Forest
by Kaylee Keech

As I walk through the dreary, dark rain forest
I look around at all the magnificent things there are to see
Trees growing taller than skyscrapers
Vines swaying in the wind
Rain pouring fast to the ground
Then I see a jaguar lurking around, on the prowl
It spots something and leaps
It eats and is contented for the night
As I head back for my plane
I recall everything that happened that day
The marvelous creatures
And I hope I can someday come back

Myrtle and Swish
by Laura Kerestes

There once was a turtle who was named Myrtle
She was friends with a fish and his name was Swish
They did everything together and promised to be friends forever
They went on a vacation and Swish was impatient
So Swish got lost and the train had a cost
And he couldn't go home so he was stuck in Rome
Myrtle got worried so she hurried
She wanted to see her friend Swish, the Siamese fighting fish
When they were reunited, they were excited
To be together again and that is the end

Horses
by Kara Marshner

I heard the horses neigh
I jumped on a horse
Rode with the ocean's
Winds
Felt as if I were flying
I hope that day will come true someday

My Protector
by Elizabeth Gable

Your love makes my heart go boom, boom, boom
My love is always right
My love is never wrong
She keeps me goin' strong
She is never wrong
She is always right
Her love is bound on me like the darkness of the night
Every day and every night
I think of her in my book of rights, her and her only
To me, her love is the greatest thing
She is the one I treasure and the one I love
And will love forever and ever for life
Her love makes my heart go boom, boom, boom!

Shooting Stars
by Eleanor Hatch

Shooting stars
Glittering, flickering
Zooming across the sky
Zip! Zap!
They're gone

It's Spring
by Madison Kroner

The flowers are blooming
From a bud to a flower
It's spring! It's spring!
The birds are growing
From an egg to a beauty
It's spring! It's spring!
The weather is getting warmer
Warmer and warmer
It's spring! It's spring!
Say goodbye to the jackets
And hello to the t-shirts
It's spring! It's spring!
Although it's not winter or summer
It's spring! It's spring!

Summer Fun
by Stephanie Connell

Summer is a wonderful time
There are barbecues and pools
Everything is so wonderful
No one is in school
How I love summer
Swimming is very fun
Especially when you're at the beach
Just watch out for that sun!
Barbecues with your family
Are just the way to go
Picnics are the perfect place
Just make sure no one's slow!
I love vacations too
Especially when they're far from home
Go there with all your family
Just don't forget your comb!
This is why I love summer
Because it is so great
I can reassure you
There's nothing you should hate

The Beach
by Samantha Sensenig

Seagulls flying
Children playing
Waves crashing
Children splashing
Building sand castles
Finding seashells
Kites flying
So high in the sky
Boats sailing
So far in the distance
Picnic lunch
Bathing in the sun
Tired children
A day of fun

Fall
by Duncan Ziants

Fall is
Awesome
Leaves are sometimes
Light yellow

My Puppy, Lucky
by Shawnee Hamilton

Licker
Unbelievable
Cute
Kind
Yelper

Zack
by Zachary Streno

Zero percent unkind
Adventurous person
Courageous person
Kids around with friends

Spring
by Amber Nimal

Spring showers
Pouring
Rain
Instead of snow
Nice flowers start to
Grow!

Chris
by Christopher Elish

Can play the trombone
Has a good puppy
Reconsiders a lot
Ice cream is the best
Satisfies himself by watching TV

Frogs
by Ashley Coyle

Friendly little creatures
Ribbiting everywhere
Oh, there are so many colors I see
Green, blue, orange, red, and purple
Small, colorful, wonders of the world

Honesty
by Samantha Adams

Honesty is a very good thing
Openness can happiness bring
Never tell a lie, always speak the truth
Everyone knows lying is uncouth
Saying what they think sometimes breaks the ice
Truthfulness is always nice
You can always make friends without paying the price

Horses
by Briana Dingler

Heartwarming
Overwhelming
Rapid
Soft
Energetic
Swift

My Loving Family
by Emily Chabalie

Many faces
Yelling and having fun

Looking out for one another
Open minds
Very funny
Into watching sports
Never failing
Getting together

Future generations
Always close by
Many friends to depend on
I love them all
Lots of questions
Your secret's safe with us

Mackenzie
by Mackenzie Zemba

Math is my favorite subject
Always prepared for class
Can do really hard multiplication problems
Kenzie is my nickname
Excellent
Nice to my friends
Zemba is my last name
Illieanna is my friend
Excited to see my friends every day

If Doom Left
by Jessica Barwell

As I walked in the graveyard that night
I could feel that I would have a great fright
The deeper I went into the darkness

I saw blackness
Felt scared

Dreamed of a way to escape this horror
On the roof of an abandoned house, I sat
Ogres of doom raised through my head
Millions of skeletons rising from the dead

Left my thoughts
Eventually, I woke from my nightmare
Fell back to sleep
Then awoke, back in the graveyard once more

Spring
by Justynne Carsten

Spring time
Pride
Ready
In time for
No
Good day!

Easter
by Dylan Tressler

Eggs are brightly colored
Always filled with treats
Searching in the yard
That will be so neat
Easter is so fun
Running in the grass

Essence
by Essence Henderson

Essence
Smart, knows the answers with special things to say
Special, like a pearl found in a clam
Educated, learning different things and by going to school
Nice, by speaking nicely to people and not screaming at them
Commuter, I travel like a train
Enthusiastic, always in a hurry

Harey Henry
by Mikayla Conant

Hairy dog
Awesome dog
Rolls a lot
Excited dog
Yelps a lot

He is brown
Easy to get rid of
Not bad
Runs a lot
Yellow is his favorite color

Moving On
by Hannah Ewald

Do you know what happened when you left me in the dust?
My heart grew cold and numb, then slowly began to rust
All of this happened to me because you didn't care
I could no longer let love in, it was too much to bear
The world is now my enemy, it's no longer my friend
I really want to be strong, so I can love again
I'm picking up the pieces to my broken heart
So many memories come to mind, I just don't want to start
Someday I will be strong again, you just wait and see
Sometime I will love again, and be who I'm meant to be

My Friend, My Sister
by Meghan Holzer

I met this girl at dance one day
Now my friend, in my heart she will stay
We are nearly the same, sisters you might say
Always having fun in so many ways
She told me one day she met this boy
He sounded nice, she was filled with joy
However, you see, I was very wrong
He was into drugs and was all along
I told my friend that it had to end
He wasn't for her, she didn't listen, not to me
I tell her I worry for her everyday
I tell her I care too much to let him treat her in that way
I reminded her often of the worry that I feel
Always hopping that she will end the whole ordeal
I talk to her again, though many days have passed
Now ready to listen, she sees that it can't last
She decided to leave him, it takes a lot of strength
She knows that I am with her, at any length
I met this girl at dance one day
Forever my sister, in my heart she will stay

The Laughter of Angels
by Saul Díaz

The sands of time are slipping
The clock won't stop ticking
The clouds are slowly drifting
Into a new dimension
Man's mortal destiny is near ...
For the end, we all fear
As the stars burn out, one by one
The heavens will clear
Look upon a mirror ...
The lights have grown dimmer ...
While the angels lay upon darkening clouds
Laughter is the only sound

Alexa Kane

Alexa is a girl of many talents.
In addition to being an avid reader and writer,
this busy fourth grade student serves as
student senate representative for her class.
She is also a member of Girl Scouts,
and even performs in various school plays.
Her poem, "A Peaceful Place" is like a breath of fresh air,
as refreshing as the special day it describes.

A Peaceful Place
by Alexa Kane

The lilacs smell sweet
And the daisies smell delightful
Just the kind to put in a vase
It's one big garden
With the sun's rays shining golden streaks across the pond
And a frog upon a lily pad
It is sitting almost happily, cleaning its toes
I rest on the bench, giggling away
With a butterfly on my nose
Then it flies to a tulip and sucks the sweet nectar down
When I realize there is no better place than here

2nd Place

Giridhar Srinivasan

When asked to describe a recent cruise,
most people will describe a series of events.
What separates Giridhar, is the ability to convey to the reader
the euphoria of being completely immersed
in the surrounding splendor,
and the overwhelming effect on the senses.
Very impressive poetry from this fifth grade student.

The Midnight Sun
by Giridhar Srinivasan

Feeble aurora;
The midnight sun
A drowsing family on a silent cruise ship
No soul awake, except one
I prance from my bed
Head clogged with dreamy imaginations
Fantasies
Glimmering ocean
Glaring sun
The landscape awes me
The light captures me with its solid stare
Its dazzling power
I clamber to bed;
The light has set fire to my mind

1st
Place

Manasa Atyam

Manasa was in the fifth grade
when selecting a poem to submit
to the America Library of Poetry,
although the inspiration for the work
may have come from an earlier time.
"First Days" speaks
to a very alienating experience,
which unfortunately,
is all too common in today's society.

First Days
by Manasa Atyam

Behind my back, soft words pass from mouth, to ear
Soon the whispers flow in the gentle wind to my lonely spot

As they pass, they drop those painful selfish words
They go down my back leaving shivers
They go through my stomach leaving butterflies

Soon they reach their destination: my heart
As they pass they leave a mark, one that I will never forget

So tightly it clutches that ball of feelings
Breaking it into a million pieces
Not knowing where to go they stay inside of my miserable body

From time to time they whisper
And make me remember
The me that used to sit alone
On the days I first started school

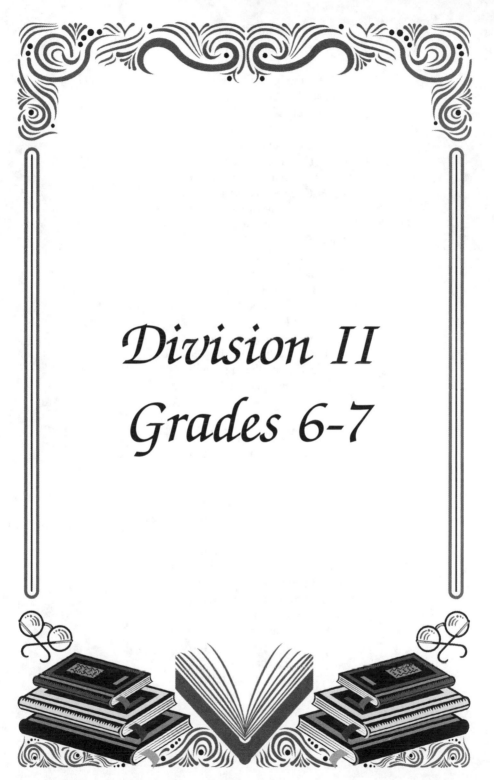

Division II
Grades 6-7

The Flower
by Shane Magee

Near the bridge there is a stream
Near the stream there is a flower
Its beauty is of nothing I can deem
Its essence is of awesome power
The taste is a different tale
The juice is enough to kill
The petals will make one ail
One seed is enough to ill
The evil is invisible to mortal eyes
Its flattery is charm
Praise from it will lead only to demise
Intending personal gain and harm
The one drawn to the flower is a fool
He means nothing to it at all
For he is used only as a tool
But still to the flower he'll call
All who are drawn are used
The man from the flower fled
Guaranteed the latter will lose
And metaphorically is dead

The Tony Award Winner
by Caterina Cutenese

Performing, choreographing, vocalizing, composing
Idina Menzel, one of my favorite actresses
Choreographing the different dances
Learning the famous songs
Staging the comical moves
Gathering the stunning costumes
Finally: it's opening night!
Inexperienced actors and actresses
Go to Idina for acting tips
Absolutely amazing audition advice
Stunning staging tips
Very vital vocal skills
Chorus blending techniques

Veteran's Day
by Hannah Skiff

I wish you could come home from Iraq
I am worried there will be an attack
I wish you were free so you could roam
Then after the war we could send you home
You could come home and be safe and sound
With your kids you could play around
Every veteran would be nice and warm
No longer would anyone need to mourn
On your way home you stop at a door
They give you milk and cookies; you want more
When you arrive, you can see your wife
You are now at home with a whole new life!

Monsters Lurking In the Night
by Erika Fenstermaker

Have you ever wondered what makes that bang in the night?
It most likely is a monster in the night
Your parents tell you, "Don't be a fright"
"There is no such thing as a monster in the night"
You tell them you heard something in the attic
They tell you, "Don't get spastic"
"There is just dust in the attic"
Nine chances out of ten
You're wrong again
But you ask
"When did you check that attic last?"
So when you hear a noise in the night
And you think it is a monster stretching to its full height
Do not get a fright
Because nine chances out of ten
You'll be wrong again

The Veterans and Me
by Ryan Allen

The Veterans and I sit in a tree
I thank them and they thank me
I say I support them across the sea
Just the Veterans and me
And then I have to say goodbye
I said it's time for me to fly
The sun is setting in the sky
"Goodbye to the Veterans," said I

A Recipe For an Uncle
by Cheyenne Poole

Take 2 cups of a gentle man
Add 2 cups of a caring person
And add 3 cups of a father figure
Mix in a blender until you see a handsome man
Pour in a love pan
Cook in a heart at 500 degrees until tan
You can tell he's done when he hugs you and kisses you
Let stand till you hear him tell you, "I love you"
Sprinkle on some best friend ever
Serve with your hugs
Taste the best uncle

I Miss You
by Kalee Kratovil

Whenever I smell my grandpa's coffee
I know he is back from working on the field
I'm in the kitchen talking away, while he sits and listens
Both of us eating Grandma's chocolate chip cookies
But that's not my story
My story is, my grandpa is getting sick
Doctors say there's nothing they can do
Month after month, hoping he stays alive
Until … Christmas Eve night, he dies

Tiptoe
by Emily Tressler

Tiptoe sneaks behind
During a dark night
Tiptoe creeps on you
Timing is right
Tiptoe prowls toward
Sure she's not noticed
Tiptoe, the best
Being silentest, slowest

Fly
by Marisela Poblete

I'm so jealous of those birds that fly
Up, up, oh, so high in the sky
They soar over the clouds
Nice, big, and loud
If only I could do the same
But down here on Earth, drives me insane
When they're chirping, I know they are mocking me
I just want to cry and flee
I dream of flying everyday and night
I can see it now and it's such a wonderful sight!
If only God gave me wings
He could see my beautiful talented things
Those birds want to make me scream
They are, oh, so mean
I just want to fly
Through the puffy, white clouds in the sky
I try everyday and every night
To climb that tree and take my flight
One day I'll fly
Up, up, oh, so high in the sky

My Mom
by Zimare Gesesse

My mom is a beautiful star
She gives love to other people
Her eyes are beautiful and her smile, too
She is as smart as a lion
She solves people's problems
She knows many things that I don't know
My mom is a funny monkey
She makes people laugh and love her
She does very funny things
My mom is a crazy animal
She does what other people don't do
She is very strong
She is a sweet chocolate cake
She helps people and cares for people

Tornado
by Michael Murphy

The leaves danced lightly in the breeze
But then they started to pick up speed
The trees suddenly bowed down
And I looked to the sky with a frown
As the tornado began to spin 'round and 'round

The Beyond
by Cody Larson

Out there, somewhere
There is love …
Beyond the hills, mountains, and beyond the sky
There is hope …
Beyond the ground, dust, and matter itself
There is happiness ...
Beyond air and beyond infinity
There are poems ...
Beyond the beyond
There is life

My Nanna
by Alliyaha Kimbrough

My nanna is the strongest, most beautiful woman you will ever know
If she had a choice to stay or go, she would have stayed, even if for one more day
But God had other plans for His child
He loves her as much as we do
And did not want to see her in pain and suffering any longer
We must all admit that my nanna's fight was a hard one, but she withstood it all
I am so proud of her for how well she handled her illness
Sometimes we can be selfish and cry; we say we didn't want her to go
But we all know that she is in a better place now
I know that when I get sad, my nanna is not far away
My nanna is looking down from Heaven upon me and you
She will always be in my heart and in my memories
Nanna, I miss you and I love you

My Family
by Lauren Deliman

My family is the Trevi Fountain
My mom is the magical wishing coins at the bottom
Always wishing the best for us
My brother is the water that never stops going
My friends are the structure that holds the fountain together
I am the amazing sound of the water dripping down the stone

Horses
by Megan Jones

Horses are for dreamers that dream of beautiful creatures
You can ride horses in cotton fields and relax
You can always talk to horses because they feel your pain and sorrow
Horses are animals that help you get to Heaven by calming you
When you look into a horse's eyes, you feel at peace with the world
When you're sad, you should watch a horse run and buck, and be free
Like Midnight and Bear, the horses would help people
And be gentle to my mom when she was going to die
Horses have an amazing sense
You can learn a lot about them and they learn from you

I've Known
by Thanh-Xuan Tran

I've known my grandparents' house
I've known those prosaic colors of wallpaper
And those rickety, elegant, curved stairs, leading to a new door every time
Always seeking new adventures and retaining old memories
Having fun and doing new stuff with your elders
Chasing scrawny chickens, around the open backyard, when twilight falls
Having fun and helping cook dinner with your elders, with a smile on
Hearing stories about you, when you were a young kid
I've known my grandparents' house
The place where you can learn new things
Always seeking new adventures and retaining old memories

Shocky
by Jacob Arnold

There was a boy named Shocky
He would always act so jocky
If you're wondering why this is his name
You are sure to get shockied

Creature
by Kyla Edwards

Back in the dark corner
Lurks a blue and red, fierce, little creature ...
Back, forth it glides
At the bottom of its
Rectangular box
Staring you down
Waiting for grub
Then light turns on
He lets his guard down
As it feasts through the night

Dear Mommy
by Cheyenne Michel

Through these years I've been here
I've dealt with a ton of pain and fear
Most of all because of you
I've had to be dealt with and put through
So many times I've seen you cry
To lay there and slowly die
Through these years I've been through this
You're the same spiraling abyss
Still with the drinking and the hate
You still ask, "Why?" about this fate
You may always regret
But you can't take back the grief I've met
Through these years I've been here
Matters have changed and I've lost fear
No reason to run and to hide
Now with Daddy by my side
And yes, Mommy, this is for you
I can never fix this heart you broke in two

Pencil Case
by Megan Barnett

My family is a pencil case
My mom is the eraser, fixing our mistakes
My dad is the ruler, keeping us all in line
My sister is the pencil, always willing to help
My brother is the pen, not always able to fix his mistakes
I am the highlighter, bringing out the color and strong points of the family

The Rockslide of My Life
by Daniel Yoders

My family is a rockslide
My grandpa is the rain that starts the slide
My grandma is the rock falling to the ground
My mom is the ground that absorbs the impact
I am the car that gets crushed by the rocks

Florida Beach
by David Schummer

Palm trees were swaying in the air
As fish swam underwater
The waves splashed loudly in my head
And loud birds squawked above me
The ocean breezes were salty in my nose
With the sourness of citrus along with it
The warm tropical water on my hand was refreshing
And the beach sand is soft on my feet
The fresh air, crisp in my mouth
The taste of oranges not far behind it
And, relaxed as could be, I felt calm

Rainbow
by Gema Gutierrez

Let them be as colorless as they want
Always gloomy and melancholy
But let them be captured and locked in a cage
I'd rather be a stunning and multicolored rainbow
Let me be free to roam the robin blue sky
Let me color the faces of the sad
To bring joy on a chaotic day
To bring summer when it's spring
To decorate the clear and plain sky
I'd rather be a jubilant rainbow than a washed-out cloud
If I could be glamorous or magnificent
I'd rather be a rainbow

What If?
by Tyler Ueke

What if you got hit by a door?
What if you got kicked by a boar?
What if you got hit in the knee?
What if you got stung by a bee?
What if you got hit in the face?
What if you got in last place?
What if your car exploded?
What if your stomach imploded?

Jess
by Rachel Tunender

When I watch you laughing at my jokes when I'm not even making any
Or when I see you with a colossal smile on your face
And sharing time for fun together
When I hear you talking about friends, family
Or that new puppy you are going to get
I say you are a best friend, through all we've been through
You are the best friend a girl can ever have!

Shore To Shore
by Janessa Arnold

There was a "family fight"
So dreadful, so many nights
But the men kept fighting on
Fighting, fighting on
That long and dreadful war
Helped shape us all the more
For our country
From shore to shore

My Perfect Angel
by Kayla Stumpf

She whirls all around me, she sleeps right beside me
With her soft and beautiful wings, wondering if she uses strings
She whispers in my cold, dreadful ear; when I get that sign that fear is near
She never leaves me, day or night
Which lets me know, I can't go down without a fight
She's my sunny day, with brightness all around
She's my heart, when it can't be found
She's the sunset setting after dawn
She's every butterfly that's on my lawn
She's a thousand stars in the midnight sky
She's every wind you see blow and fly
She's my perfect angel, so soft and so sweet
She's my angel that will never leave my side or completely fleet away
That's my perfect angel!

A Recipe For the Best Brother
by Alyshia Talmage

Take 10 cups of love and care
Take 1/2 cup of meanness
7 cups of he takes me everywhere
Put in a 2006 Chevy in Indiana, PA
Stir with a loveable heart until he's sweet
Pour into a chair
Cook in a big hug at 98.6 degrees until he's loveable
You can tell when he's done when he says, "Hello"
Add black hair, hands, and feet
Cut with coolness
Tastes like the best big brother!

The Sea
by Michael Eyler

The colorful fish
Swimming swiftly through the sea
Watch them jump so high

Teens
by Hailey Waagmeester

Let them be babies
Cuddled, fed, and diapered by their moms
I'd rather be a teen
A free teen cruising down the highway
With my sunglasses proudly upon my face
To be free to leave whenever I feel like it
If I could be carefree and independent
I'd rather be a teen

Happy and Free
by Taylor Allison

Happy and free
This is what my dreams scream
But chains and bars keep me in
Locked from the world
Happy and free
Is my only wish
I see fields of green
Skies of blue
Laughter is what I need
Happy days
Free days
They haunt me in my sleep
I will never be living
Without limitation
Happy and free
Happy and free
Is what I wish to be

The World Through a Puppy's Eyes
by Megan Duraso

Puppies smile with their eyes
With their kisses
With their cuddles
With their tails
Puppies love playing
Love chewing
Love chasing
Love you
Puppies sleep with closed eyes
Little yip-yips
Legs and tails twitching
Dreaming of bones
Puppies listen for food
For water
For treats
For an invitation to play
Puppies know how to smile
How to love
How to sleep
How to listen

Peaceful Water
by Samarra Kimmy

Watch the flowing water
Flowing as peacefully as can be
Watch the water in the morning
As it sparkles in the sunlight
Watch the water at night
For it casts a shadow upon the water
See the fishes splashing water
Whoa, look out!
See, it's as blue as can be
I think I'll go for a swim
I'll hopefully not be back after 9:00 again

The Beast That Follows Winter
by Jessica Chalfant

Spring is a savage lion, waiting all year to be unleashed
Pacing in a rage until the day it can be ceased
On that day he dominates, starting the beginning of new life
Not only the flowers and foliage, but also the wildlife
The wind whirls as though rippling his mane
As he stands strong and proud during his reign
When he bellows, his mighty breath can always be felt
Just like the warmth that caused the winter snow to melt

Midnight Symphony
by Tiffany Howard

Stars twinkle
Crickets chirp in the dew-sprinkled grass
Fireflies hum softly past my ears
Frogs croak in the clear pond
The small brook gurgles with life
The piercing cry of a hungry coyote, on the prowl
Sounds faintly in the nearby forest
Wind whistles through my open window
I hum a soft lullaby
Adding to the forte of the surrounding symphony

Our Protectors
by Alexander Carter

Our soldiers are now in war
There and now
They're in the dessert
Sweat dripping from their brow
They protect our freedom
And our rights
By making it through
These dreadful fights
They put their lives
Inside fate's hands
As they march right through
Our enemy's lands
For many mothers
It is their dread
That their precious boys
Come home dead
They face their fears
And fight America's fight
So we always hope
They come home one night

Remember Back Then
by Richelle Ayers

Do you remember back then, when gas didn't cost a lot of money
Or when people didn't have to be rude, just to be funny?
As we remember back then, we notice some things, life was easier
You didn't see kids looking down at the screens of their little machines
People weren't yelling, but they were talking together
Their pleasant conversations could go on forever and ever!
Now days, the youth have no respect
They sit in front of their color TVs
Doing something mindless for hours unending!
I remember back then when people had bright smiling faces!
I'm here to tell you my opinion about our generation!
I look back in history, then at us, and I'll sum it up
Our generation is lazy and pampered and rotten!
So my dear friends, let's remember back then, and change our lives!
For it's never too late to change back then!

R.I.P. Myron Cope
by Jason Rippole

Terrible Towel
Is a Pittsburgh legacy
Swing it 'round and 'round

Drip
by Jack DiMidio

Drip, never out of beat
He's never flowing
Always dashes to his feet
Drip stops when he's tired out
When I wake him
He's not out to pout
I find Drip in different places
In sinks, in my gutter
But one thing's for sure
He never stutters

Butterfly
by Jessica Smoker

I fly gracefully in the sun
Flapping my wings back and forth
The breeze pushes me along
As I fly high and low
My wings are like a mask
I disguise myself with them
They help me hide from my enemy
They help me catch my prey
When winter comes I hide
I fly far away; I fly to the south
I leave my home until spring comes again

Dream
by Sarah Bevilacqua

A black fog
Wrapping its arms around me
A black fog
Through it, nothing I see
A dark mist
Makes all goals come true
A dark mist
Stories unfold, big, bright, and new
A blank pallet
Repeats of previous files
A blank pallet
Only for awhile

Harley
by Becky Brickell

She waits at the stairs
Waiting for the door to open
When she hears the bus go by ...
Barking orders is what she does best
Jumping with joy she runs
Into my arms

Apollo
by Haley Justice

Apollo
Has the pride of two
Made up of me and you
His mane glows greatly, loyal and true
The day is never blue
Whether laying or playing
He's always there for you!

Oreo
by Madison Weidel

Rough, hard, bumpy
A sandwich
That melts in your mouth
Two cookies instead of bread
A chocolate delicacy
Inside you'll find a special treat
A creamy, sweet, smooth surprise
This sandwich is the best dessert
Despite its small size

Hawk
by Mollie Flowers

Hawk sitting in a tree
Hawk soaring free
Now soaring high
Having a wonderful eye
Like the humans far below
You are wishing for no sadness or woe
You no longer need a flock
Graceful, peaceful, flying hawk

Happy and Free
by Megan Risley

Happiness and freedom
Have not been mine
Since I awoke today
That horrible moment
When I'm destined to return
Return
Return to reality
Even if the dream was bad
Deep inside, I was still happy and free
Free from the fear of what others think
What you can do or what you can't
Dreams are the only truly free place
Where you can be free of others' words and thoughts
For being free can make anyone happy

Cape May
by Sam Bollinger

Delicious cheese steak odor
Wafting down the mobbed streets
Children
Laughing
Splashing
In the ice cold surf
Sizzling sand scorches
Feet as
The hot sun
Lights up
The shining
Emerald
Sea

Saturday
by Katie Myers

Today we are off to soccer for the first time
We are almost there, but I can't be on-line
Yes, we are here before the very bad fine
"Hey!" I yelled, "That's not yours, but it's mine"
"Hey Mom," I yelled running down the hill
My mom called back from the bottom of there still
"Cool, but I can't see Bill"
"Sweet, here we are, no thanks to Will!"
Well, a very special day
We are here by the bay
"Cool," we all yelled, "Come here Kay"
I yelled, "Wait it's Saturday!"

Bubblegum
by Tyla Metcalfe

Chewy like Laffy Taffy
Colorful like a rainbow
As soft as a marshmallow
Sweet like cotton candy
As small as your eye

The Hollowmazoo
by Taryn Romig

The Hollowmazoo
Oh, he scares me, he do
He has big, shiny teeth
He eats ten men for a feast
Oh, that Hollowmazoo
He's a monster, he is
When he opens his mouth
All you see is white fizz
He'll eat you whole with no questions asked
And say, after he's done
"Boy, you tasted good and I had so much fun"
Oh! That Hollowmazoo
He gives me a temper
Last summer I watched him
Eat my friend, Kemper
He's a beast, so he is
And I don't care for him much
But tomorrow I have to go meet him for lunch

In My Mind
by Collette Saez

I never really know what's going on in my head
It all starts before I get out of bed
Every day is a daily routine
Everyone stares at me like I'm a machine
But inside my head nothing's the same
Everything is a different game
Inside my head, there are things I can't explain
So I sit outside in the pouring rain
There are many interesting magical places
And millions of smiling happy faces
There are so many things people want me to be
And so many others that make up me
No one will ever know what goes on in my mind
Until the one day that I finally shine

Till That Day
by Katherine Sims

We laughed, we played, till that day
We shared our tears, we shared our fears
Till that day
Now you're gone, he took you away on that day
I'm looking for the stairway to bring you back to me
Go back in time, relive that day, and keep you there with me
Bring you home
Everyone will be glad, they'll no longer be sad
Till that day

I Have Found
by Shelby Smeltz

Right as I hit the ground
I feel that I have found
Something that I can do
Other than tie my shoe
Everyone sits and cheers
Even though it hurts their ears
I jump up
Once again
And then smile
At my friend

Dreams
by Kayla Moss

I'm lying there all night, trying to dream
But all that comes up was myself counting sheep
After I count the sheep, somehow I start to be a frog
So then, I start to leap, leap, leap!
I'm lying there all night trying to dream
Something pops up and a horse comes and licks me
So I jump and the horse takes a ride
While I'm on there saying, "Go faster!"
Finally, the next day comes
And I wake up and I blurt out
"That was some crazy dream!"

A Day In Real Life
by Brittany Tilkens

I'm sad, mad, and very bad
If I only knew my dad
You mistake me for a cad
If I only knew my dad
My mom is gone, she's gone to me
I wonder if I'll ever be
Mother of a healthful three
I wonder if I'll ever be
My brother left
With grand theft
Packed his bags with a heft
With another grand theft
Brother two in trouble
Just got in another rumble
He mumbled
"Just another rumble"
I wish not to offend
Or my relationships to bend
I only wish to mend
The hearts of those at wits' end

Bio-Poem
by Kali Wentling

I wish I could play the piano
Like the five Brown's
And I dream of crazy, wild songs
I am playing with other parts of my body that aren't my hands
I used to tap the beat with my feet
But now I am living the dream
I seem to show my true talent
But I'm really showing me

The Wait
by Amber Lantz

I'm waiting, waiting for someone to take me home
People come in every once and a while
But no one seems to want me
Every morning I wake up and another dog is gone
I heard that if you're there for a while or there is not enough room
They will put you to sleep, and you never ever wake up
I've been here for a while ... my days could be limited

My House
by Zealan LaCombe

The beautiful house
Protects us with its great strength
And won't be beaten

My Dog
by Linnea Rudy

I have a dog named Cheyenne
She loves to bother you
She loves to be center of attention
She responds when I call, "Puppy boo"
She loves to be outside
So she watches the clock
She waits for us to get home; when we do
She says, "Finally, now let's go for a walk"
She likes to be with our neighbor's dogs
They always push and play
When she comes home, she is tired
So she goes to the couch and lays
If we ever have a bad day
She runs and kicks
We are always surprised
How much she loves to lick

I Miss You
by Emily Benfer

Since you're gone
I miss you all the time
You used to call me your angel
From fooling around
To working together
From helping with the chores
To getting dirty in the garden
From the Korean War
To driving around in a milk truck
You were always there for me
And always will be
And even though you're not here
I miss you all the time
The good times we spent together
It's just that ...
I didn't have the chance to say good-bye

From a Leaf's Point of View
by Mariana Riehl

I'm green, sometimes red
Just hanging on the trees
Up in the air, up on the trees
Nothing to do but hang here, waiting
Waiting to fall
It starts to get cold
I'm starting to turn red
I start to wither up
I'm falling down to the ground
Why do I have to get raked into a pile?
Why do I have to get jumped on?

Love That Friend
by Jacinda Zook

Love that friend
Like a frog loves flies
I said I love that friend
Like a frog loves flies
Love to listen to my friend
Love to call my friend in the wind
"Hey there, friend!"

I Said I Hate That Potato
by Matthew Martin

Hate that potato
Like oil and water
I said I hate that potato
Like school and a kid
Hate to eat him at supper
Hate to eat him
"Hate you, potato"

I Am the Wind
by Arizona Bitler

I am the wind
You know me for rushing through your hair
My mother, speed
My father, peace
I was born in your heart, free, wild, but yet tame
I live in you
My best friend is life, where I can show off my talents
My enemy is summer, where I can barely move
I fear space where I cannot roam, but be stuck with rushing rocks
I love being free, to roam anywhere I please to
I wish of being everywhere at once to rush through
But yet, peaceful with you ... and you ... and you!

Summer
by Shannon Leland

Summer is a time of relaxation, playing, and little worries
A time away from school and studies
A time to figure out life and the future
To make friends and feeling like you've always known him or her
And not always having to be on your best behavior
Treating others how you want to be treated and asking nothing in return
Being an example of Jesus everywhere you turn
Not knowing what will happen next, but looking forward to it anyway
Being able to forgive others, no matter what they say
Having an open heart and mind
Being devoted and kind
Not forgetting how loved you are
Knowing that God is not very far
Putting your selfishness and pride away
Going through struggles and knowing it will be okay
Doing your best in everything you do, even if it is hard
Not hesitating to go on, but just playing life like a card
Cherishing every moment, and everyone who steps in and out of your life
Even if you go through anguish and strife
Summer is a time of wonder, and just a time to live our lives

What Happens To a Dream Deferred
by Mallory Garcia

What happens to a dream deferred?
Does it burst like a bubble
Or soak up like a sponge?
Does it sink like a rock
Or float like a boat?
Maybe it blows out like a light
Or does it dissolve like snow?
Maybe it just drifts away like a river!

Pipe Cleaners
by Tyler Rea

Pipe cleaners, pipe cleaners
O what you can make
Make no mistake
Not childish or silly
Not willy or nilly
Just simple and straight
No reason to hate
O what you can make
Places, animals, people galore
Anything that lives shore to shore
Plants and ants
Hats or bats
Or even a snake
O what you can make
With pipe cleaners, pipe cleaners

Run With Me
by Kelsie Boose

Run with me Daddy
Run to the end of the rainbow
I have a lot to learn
So just run, run with me Daddy, we can fix it
You can teach me more when we're at the end
Daddy, run with me to the end
Then we can fly the rest of the way
Daddy, run with me please
So in the end we can fly
Fly up, up, up, and up till we reach the sky
And you'll be with me, forever and all the time

Untitled
by Elizabeth Monahan

Freedom is like a bird
Flying over an ocean
That never falls down
Gliding over land made of freedom
Freedom is in every place
But most of all we are freedom

Limerick
by Rachael Brizes

A very fat cow
He wanted to lose weight, but how?
He started to run
But he gained a ton
He finally gave up and ate his towel

Angel Has Fallen
by Javier Garcia-Perez

An angel has fallen to the ground from the sky
The angel is the one that protects you in sad and happy times
Angel of lost hopes and angel of love in sad and happy times
Angel who is there for you and angel who encourages you like your friends
Your friends are like angels, who brighten your days
In all kinds of wonderful ways
Their thoughtfulness comes as a gift from above from the sky
And we feel we're surrounded by warm, caring love
Like upside down rainbows, their smiles bring the sun down to the ground
And they fill out moments with humor and funny times with laughter and fun
Friends are like angels without any wings
Blessing our lives with the most precious things
They can't fly high or take us up to the sky
But they are there for you in lovely times
Now I pray, Dear Father who is in Heaven
Please bless this child christened this day in your holy name
With the love and care of your perfect way
Please bless this guardian angel to watch over this precious day
And protect this innocent child with your loving care
To be forever safe and always close to you

Grandmother
by Jessie Apgar

Love is like a gift
So caring and true
You were like an angel
Who helped me carry through
I'm hoping and praying to see you again
I'll miss you to the very end
Still seeing the shadows of you by my bed
But as I lay down my head
You seem to disappear again
I've lost my best friend, she is gone
Sometimes I feel so alone
My beloved grandmother is happy in Heaven
And when she left me
She was only ninety-seven

Autism: Intersecting Worlds
by Chris Besser

Long ago when I was three, I wanted my brother to play with me
What I couldn't comprehend, is why he wouldn't be my friend
I would often ask my parents why, and both of them would then reply
Trapped in a world of autism, he seems to be; is he there eternally?
I would often see my parents tear, because this world they did fear
Separated from the world he would be, with little connection to reality
Everyday my parents would attempt to guide
From within his disconnected world inside
With this battle would we lose or win, standing outside looking in
Years have passed and words are still very few, but he can communicate with you
A picture symbol, a tug or a glance, or a random word by chance
My brother may not have a choice, so I have learned to be his voice
But autism could not erase, the feeling I see etched upon his face
When normal milestones are missed, those who love and care for him must resist
If we concentrate on what will never be, progress, even slow, we'll never see
It is absolutely no disgrace, for his differences to embrace
Even though who he is, we will always adore
We will always attempt to strive for something more
To the outside would his differences are clear
But things aren't always as they appear
To those who view him with chagrin, miss the beauty that lies within
Others have called him a "cross to bear", but my parents reply, "Au, contraire"
Both of them and I surmise, he is a blessing in disguise

The Way People Look
by Brooke Soper

Some people think
Life is unfair
But all they want
To do is stare
They're to look away
But they just look and look
In some weird way
And just to say
They are ashamed

I've Known
by Garrett York

I've known Calumet, Iowa
Where everybody knows everybody
Whenever someone drives by, you wave to them as if a family member
It's so small, you can walk all the way across town in a breeze
We always go see Grandma and the shop
Where Grandpa worked on beat up, rusted cars
Now we use it for our own use, like the boat
I've known Calumet, Iowa

Come With Me
by Samantha Toft

Come with me to the farm
See the horses running over the soft, green grass in the meadow
Hear the hoofbeats over the soft earth
Smell the fresh air, as rain clouds cover the sky above
Taste the clear well water coming from the soft earth
Feel the cool, gentle raindrops soften the earth, as the clouds cry
Come with me to the farm of wonders

A Dream Deferred
by Marin VanRoekel

What happens to a dream deferred?
Does it mold like bread and dry out
Or sting like a bee and then fly away fast?
Does it stink like sweaty feet
Or crust like a booger hanging out of your nose?
Maybe it's just there to hang out, like a spider
Or does it zip away with a smile
And never come back?
-Inspired by Langston Hughes

Crush
by Rachel Kramer

When you gaze at me
I have butterflies inside
And my heart takes flight
Your presence makes me waver
When you leave, I die

Heartbroken
by Becky Kokltus

The night he broke my heart
It hit me like a dart
I broke down and cried
Knowing I had tried
He chose her instead of me
She just rubbed it in my face with glee
I know he didn't care
I know he knew it wasn't fair
I'm over it now
I truthfully don't see how
Although I pushed it out of my life now
It feels like it's still there somehow
I'm gluing my heart back together
Although a scar will be there forever
The night he broke my heart
It hit me like a dart

Mom
by Alyssa Ashcroft

Through thick and thin, I need you
I don't have to look far
You are right beside me
When I fall on the ground
Through thick and thin, you love me
No matter what I do wrong
I always say I'm sorry
And run to your loving arms
Through thick and thin, you help me
Get through obstacles in my life
No matter the height of the mountain
You are willing to climb
Through thick and thin, you listen
To everything I say
I know your ears are open
And I blab away
Through thick and thin, I love you
And I always will
You are always there for me
As I will be for you

Where I'm From
by Marcus Meston

I am from the warm summer nights with my family and friends
I'm from the grass stains that were on my pale jeans
I'm from the pink, vibrant, sunsets during August nights
I'm from Dairy Delight, the prime reason I eat ice cream
I'm from Mom's spaghetti sauce that dribbles down my chin
I'm from Nina and Tom, the extraordinary and concerning
I'm from Savannah, the vicious, but loving dog
That chased me through the neighborhood
I'm from bonfires that came and went, with friends and family together
I'm from wispy, freezing winters and cool, crisp autumns
I'm from the ocean that pulled me in and out like a rag doll
And sunburns on my face
I'm from the fish I pulled in with all my might
That fed all 12 people on my dad's side of the family
I am from all my memories that keep me happy when I am down

Friends
by Hannah Spelbring

My friends are close to me, we run and play
My friends and I, we run around trying to catch butterflies
We hang out in malls and at football games
We tell each other what is bothering us
We tell them our deepest, darkest secrets
We laugh together and we cry together
When one friend hurts, we all hurt
My friends are close to me, we run and play
My friends are close to me, and that makes me feel good

The Puddle
by Jacob Dinsmore

Lying here motionless
Destined to stay in one spot for long periods of time
My face as gray as the sky
My body as smooth as glass
I am young
A small boy running toward me
Heading to the baseball game
Getting closer and closer until suddenly ...
Splash!
I am young no longer
My face covered in wrinkles

My Puppy
by Drew Duffel

Oh, my puppy Shaft
How you run so fast
You are so cool
But everywhere, you do leave drool
Everywhere I look
From your teeth with a hook
Everything is ripped
When you first came home into my house, you oh, so tripped
Oh, my puppy Shaft
You're the best dog for which I asked

Birds Wonder
by Alexis Valko

You see birds fly
Across the sky
And where do they go
Nobody knows
They fly in flocks
Around the blocks
They have beautiful wings
And they land on swings
They make pretty nests
That are the best
When they see people they scream with glee
And then they flee
When it is time
Birds fly in a line
They make sure it's right
To take a flight
They fly in the sun
And like to eat buns
When they go back to their homes
They sing pretty tones

The Drug We Call Love
by Christina Case

The itchy feeling that quavers inside
Begging to come out
Screaming in your head
To just go do it
Do it, do it
Little voices whisper
Mimicking your every sound
They snicker
Telling you what to do
How to do it
You're fighting back the urge
This is all just deliberation turning into temptation
Crying to you to go
Crying, and yelling, and punching, and anger, and hurt, and confused
They're all actions that are normal symptoms
Of this drug we call love

Scared
by Jasmine Yeigh

I'm all alone in my room; I close my eyes but I can still see
The horrors that followed me, wherever I went
Weird noises, strange men, Mom going missing again
I looked frantically everywhere I could but I couldn't find her
I tried her cell, no answer
I was scared; I didn't know what to do
I couldn't breathe; I couldn't see
I was falling to the ground, then I woke up
I was lying on my bed, drenched with sweat
My mom was standing beside me
It was just another bad dream

My Mother
by Samantha Pritts

I love my mother
She's like no other
She makes me happy when I am sad
Although she sometimes gets mad
She makes the sun shine
She is all mine
Her hair is brown
It flows down
She is never unfair
I love her care
She helps me through tough times
She never whines
Words can't express the feelings in my heart
She is so smart
She never leaves
She always achieves
She treats me right
We hardly ever fight
We will never be torn apart
I love her heart

My First Real Friend
by Molly Nicholson

I met her when I moved
And we became friends
I met her in preschool
We were then best friends
I met her in the classroom
And we giggled at stupid things
I met her in the lunch room
When we would make faces
I met her in the summer
When we ran through the sprinklers
I met her at the lake
Where we splashed each other
I met her at her house
Where we sat and did nothing
But will we do all these things
When we're much more older?

Grandfather
by Lucas Betterton

There once was a great man
He made you feel good with the touch of his hand
With that pleasant smile
Seeing him was worthwhile
I miss seeing his wrinkled face
Watching him die was hard to embrace
Death like a spear
Made him not here
And I openly shed my tears
But now he stands at Heaven's gate
And oh, how I hate the wait
He and I had endless fun
But my time with him is long gone
In my eyes he did not falter
This great man was my grandfather
And even though his life came to an end
I'll replay our memories again and again

The One Who Only Finds the Good
by Alexandra Doyle

He lay upon my chest
Slowly, deeply breathing
Our hearts softly beating in unison with a warm flow of love
His eyes are of deep brown that show only of kindness and loyalty
The hair that bears him is only the outside making
His inside reflects the true and soft in him
His love that he holds
The kindness he sends to other living things
He is the one that truly has no care for what people look like
Or how they act
He only finds the good in people
But as he lay upon my chest
Slowly, deeply breathing
Our hearts softly beating in unison with a warm flow of love
I lie here and ponder
Why can't we all be loving and kind to one another?

Dreamin'
by Allye Tenney

My heart beats relentlessly
Skipping a beat every now and then
My life is full of meaning
Meaning I have yet to figure out
Yet in this world of dreams
Anything seems possible
But in reality
Life's just a dream that you control

The Little Blue Flea
by Austin King

There once was a little blue flea
Who lived on a funny pine tree
The wind blew
And the flea flew
And landed on a very hairy knee

Good Old Hockey Game
by Kyle Williams

Starts with the drop of the puck
Players skating and hitting
Bobby scores
Somebody roars
Good Old Hockey Game
Horn blows for the end of the 3rd period
The home team wins
The Good Old Hockey Game

The Big One
by Andrew Zundel

The feel of the wave
The control of my board
I can just feel it
The time has come for the one giant wave
The one I've been waiting for my whole life
Here it comes, my dream is about to come true
I'm on top of the world and I feel free
It's just me, my board, and the wave
My dream has come true
I have ridden the big one

The Heart of New York
by Alyssa Schimpf

As I sit down waiting for inspiration to strike
I think about what I want to do with my life
Bustling streets and busy crowds
How my creative barriers will just tumble down
I smirk as I imagine doing this years in the future
An artist's dream, I think with glee
It would be the perfect life for me
Now filled with inspiration
I come back to the present to work on my art
And I know that I'll always love what is happening now
Deep down in my heart

Forevermore
by Joscelyne Gonzalez

I am myself forevermore
I wonder what my awaiting future will be
I hear the melodious music of ballet
I see the perplexing Eiffel Tower someday
I want to explore the extraordinary deep sea
I am myself forevermore
I imagine an exotic place where there's a frantic dinosaur
I feel like I'm battling in a futile war
I touch enough like a diminishing, melancholic star
I worry about unspeakable accidents in a car
I cry when leaving love so far
I am myself forevermore
I understand life will never be fair
I say to always be aware
I dream to one day have it all
I try to be someone's wake-up call
I hope to one day feature my own brand at the mall
I am myself forevermore

The Second That Mattered
by Laura G. Brestensky

On the bus on December 1st of 1955
Segregation would have an attempted deprive
A woman so strong would say no
When she was asked to move to the back although
A white man wanted the seat she was in
And he wasn't about to let a black girl win
She was arrested and humiliated, it's true
But what she did, she would never rue
It started the boycott that was successful till it was done
And soon all black people knew they had won
All because of that one second that mattered
That ended the time Rosa Parks would be battered

Life
by Sindhura Chennupati

Grasp life when you can
If you miss, try again
Because even there before you
You miss it, is what you do
And if you miss and don't try again
Lose it, you will then
Everything you love seems to fade away
That is the price that you will pay
Without living life to the fullest
Without tasting the fine taste of tea
Without painting a room with a color you think is finest
Without tasting a fine, spicy Indian curry
So live life to the fullest
Grasp it when you can
I tell you in a way I think is gentlest
Grasp it when you can

The Stars and the Stripes
by Faith Hotchkiss

I love America's Flag
It has buried all the bold
No way it will ever sag
It makes me shine more than gold
Take for instance all the red
As more soldiers go and fight
And all of that blood is shed
Sometimes all in just one night
And take a look at the white
When Christ came to Earth and died
The pain feels like a bite
As we sit around and bide
And we can't forget about the blue
When the blood and water flowed
And then finally one day I knew
How much to Him I've owed
And of course for all those stars
Those are America's scars

Real Or Fantasy
by Katlyn Nieser

One day I met a book that could talk
And then I met a duck that could squawk
I saw a blue butterfly
And a green flower walking by
I smelled some ribs down the street
And they were shaped like some feet
Turns out they belonged to someone named Pete
I was on my way to school when I fell in a pool
And that's when I lost my cool
I started to scream; was it all a dream?
When I woke up it was 8:03
My bed was wet, oh no I overslept
And my parents had left
For breakfast I had cereal and milk
And for clothes I wore cotton and silk
I don't think I will ever go to bed
Or ever rely on my alarm clock, Ted

Hand In Hand
by Julia Dixon

Hand in hand
Heart to heart
Love is love
And truth is truth
The feelings you feel
Are the thoughts of your heart
And truth is the love in your words
The truth can sting
The truth can tickle
The way you love
And feel and express
The truth is
I love you

Flowers
by Mackenzie Sefchok

Flowers!
Roses, tulips, and daisies
No matter what they are
They are so wonderful!
No matter if they are near or far
To me they smell happy
And they look so bright
They make me feel bubbly
Even though I'm in the sunlight!
Some stand tall ...
Like sunflowers
Others are small ...
Like daisies
Flowers are ubiquitous in the spring
They seem to be everywhere
They make me want to sing
Even if I am right in front of a bear!

Child of a Soldier
by Sarah Thomas

When you hear the door close more than once
You know he's leaving again
You get a big hug, and a sad shrug
As you watch them get on the bus
Your heart starts to cry
It feels like your family's disappearing
Starting with your dad
Then you get a letter; you feel much better
Then you get a call that makes you fall to the ground
With happiness to know he's still there
Then two years later he comes in
With his uniform, so clean and neat
It is really a nice treat to see him
And when he's home, it makes me feel like a family again

Why Will You Believe?
by Brianna Frederick

Believing just blows the mind
Wondering patiently …
How? Why? When? Where?
And within each time I notice the values of each
Though the most important is, why?
As long as you believe
Everything will happen for a reason
But as some would beg to differ, they notice this statement remains superior
People use the phrase not knowing what it means
Not understanding that ...
Life ... death ... love ... and the challenge
All in each other, go hand in hand
So as we talk about wondering
Why? ...
Will you believe?

Pooh Bear and Friends
by Lauren Czerwien

Have you ever met Pooh Bear?
He has yellow fuzzy hair
He likes to eat honey and has a friend that's a bunny
He has other friends, too
Tigger, Piglet, Eeyore, and Roo
I hope you are adored and not very bored

What a Beautiful Day!
by Alessia Scoccia

The beautiful flowers gleam in the light
Oh, my! What a beautiful sight
The bright sun is shining in the sky
Then comes the birds flying by
You sigh, lying down
Looking around at all the wonderful things
God made with love
Then you look up above
God's smiling down at you
So you smile back, too!

True Love
by Haley Deibert

You brighten my day
Wherever I go
Whether it rains
Or whether it snows
You make me smile
When you're not even trying
And when I see you cry
I start crying
I miss you even when
You're standing right next to me
Your sparkling blue eyes
Are like perfect, little puddles
By the touch of your skin
I could melt into water
Our hands fit together
Like a glove
Now I know, I'm truly in love …

Red-Turned-Black Rose
by Megan Matejcic

Holding a black rose of death and despair
Tears stream down my face; I'm gasping for air
The thorns dig deep in my palms and they bleed
Down my wrists, down my arms, protesting my creed
I swear the flower was red moments ago
But without my hope, the flower can't grow
It shriveled up and withered away
Dead in my arms is where it shall stay
Are you like the red-turned-black rose?
Gone to a place that no one knows?
Where are you? Are you okay?
The last red petal has faded to grey
Are these the petals I'll lay on your deathbed?
Withered and black instead of pretty and red?
Don't end a life you have yet to complete
You have places to go, people to meet
Don't let tomorrow be your last day
Please, oh please
I want you to stay

My Pet Dog
by Jozef Turcan

Holly is a Jack Russell Terrier
Who couldn't be much merrier
Her body is quite sleek
But she is by no means meek
Her favorite thing to do is eat
She also likes to play with feet
Hiding bones in the ground
Only later to be found
When she's asleep and her eyes are shut
She is the most perfect mutt
Holly is one terrific pet
I'm so glad that we met

Graceful Turtles
by Marissa Angino

They are as full of grace
As ballerinas in a dance
The turtles glide through their home
Which is watery
The fluid motions they use
Are sometimes on pottery
Turtles today need our help
Before they disappear

Searching
by Kelsi Flinchbaugh

Lonely child left behind
The parents were not so kind
The parents were so very crude
He walks the dusty road with no shoes
He is loved by God and has no clue
He wished he had just one meal
To help his little heart heal

Blue
by Megan Adamo

Blue
Like the deepest ocean
To the farthest sky
Blue
Undulating, enveloping
Blue
Caught up in the beauty and mystery
Of this color so divine
Cannot tear my gaze away from your blue eyes
That stare right through me
Blue

How the Sunrise Had Me Thinking
by Nicole Dorn

As I step out into the bright light of the sun's rising
I begin to see beautiful shades of yellow and light orange fill the sky
No one else knows what I am feeling
But I feel as if I want to cry
While watching this amazing scene
I begin to think about all of the memories I left behind
And how my life is changing now that I am a teen
Everything I can think of is running through my mind
I realize how seeing this sunrise for the first time in my life
Actually has me in deep thought about my past
I remember all of the bad moments I've been through during this life
Then I remember all of the good times that I wanted to last
Even though I have had some ups and downs and thought that I've had enough
I never stopped reminding myself that I could always get through this all
Though times may have been rough and everything started becoming tough
I knew that I needed to stay focused on the important things most of all
I look down, then look back up again, and breathe a sigh of relief
Knowing that even though it has been difficult at certain times
I have been pretty lucky in the long run, even when I lost sight of belief
I see that the sun has risen, so I go back inside
And ponder about what I will think of next

The Peaceful Beach
by Sierra Purcell

I sit on the sandy beach
My toes curled in the moist sand
Young girls are running in the warm breeze
I smell the salty air
I walk down the glistening shore
The sun beating down on me
I throw small crumbs of bread
Seagulls race to steal the crumbs
There are families jumping over waves
Playing with a beach ball
I see a little boy digging in the sand
A beautiful, young girl building a small sand castle
The beach is so serene
I don't want to leave
But the sun is going down

Lunch Time
by Gwen Buffton

It's lunch time again and I have to choose
Where I want to sit, I win and lose
Everyday I try not to hurt
The other person's feelings, I just might burst
No matter what I choose
It seems like the whole world hates what I do
I just want to sit and eat in peace

Dreams
by David McFall

It might seem that all our dreams just won't come true
But give me time to finish this rhyme; see your dreams through
Even though (this saddens me so) odds are, no way!
With hard work and a little torque, your dreams are here to stay!
Don't forget, "It's no sweat" as long as you give your best
Soon you'll see, you're higher than me; you rise above the rest!

History Day
by Rebecca Polinski

My heart is pounding ...
I wait for the judges to say, "Begin"
I had this feeling in a competition
Called History Day
Long months of practice for a play
And it all comes down to this
Thump, thump ...
They say, "Begin" and I started to shake
The beginning, good ...
The middle, awesome ...
The end ... pure gold
The play was great!
It was the best day of my life
But ...
At the award ceremony it all changed
We didn't win or go to the state competition, but I got over it
This is because ...
All I could think about was that feeling at the end of the play
And that feeling was ...
Happy!

The Star
by Paige Cook

The man sat there preaching in the strongest tone
I had ever known
When he preaches I tend to listen well
And the raindrops drop to the bottom well
He cries when he says God is near
So listen when he is done
And watch him bear the news to the God we know
The man is the wisest to know
He lives right beside me
So I would know
That man is how old?
How should I know?
That man stares to see the world out of the corner of thine eye
Which thy father lies
But no–the man stays and looks at the stars
But why does he look at the stars?
To know he's the wisest of them all!

Underdog
by Lexie Houser

I was an underdog, who was ready to win
Standing at home plate
Waiting for the thrill to begin
Strike one! I swung too late
Bases are loaded
Pressure's on me
It felt like my heart exploded
The outfield is where the ball will be
The crowd goes wild
But the feeling so mild
I felt unbelievable
To achieve something I thought unachievable!

Gentle Mother
by Anna Kemper

Gentle is a mother's touch
Stroking her daughter's hair
Her baby's sleeping soundly
Breathing in the crisp night air
Tender thoughts whisk through her child's mind–
No limits–they cannot be confined
There are no worries
No pain, no fear
Just the pure innocence of a child so far
As she sings sweet lullabies
She thinks of what's to come–
In her hands the future lies
For her precious little one
"Good night, my dear child"
She says with a warm, loving smile
"I may be leaving you for now
But I'll be back in a little while"

Spring Is Here!
by June Grasso

Do you hear the birds chirping?
Do you smell the flowers blooming?
Do you see the sun shining so bright?
Are you planting a garden?
Did you hear?
Spring is here!

Love
by Emy Risner

Love, love is a beautiful thing
For one will last forever and ever
For one will never start
Oh, we're so close together
But we're so far apart

Looking Into the Mirror
by Morgan Lux

Looking into the mirror
But I don't see my reflection
I see an imagine I have never seen before
It's a view of a sky
But not an ordinary sky
This sky was unusual, but wonderful
It contained a cloud that was made of glass
A sun that seemed to be made of yellow crystal
A bird of many colors
There is a field of wavy grass
But as my eyes wander more, down the mirror
Something had just then caught my eye
It was someone in the mirror
This person was lying down flat on their back
On a red and white checkerboard blanket
Her eyes were gazing so deeply at the sky
It almost seemed like she was hypnotized
Just then I realized who this person was
It was me!

True Friend
by Brittani Dean

You're a true friend
I am glad I met a friend like you
You are loving and caring and outgoing too
You help me when I am down
You play with me when I am alone
You protect me from all harm
You care for me, and treat me fair in all ways
You never let me down
You shelter me
You always treat me like a sister
You are like a sister I never had
My parents like you and so do I
You are the greatest friend I ever had
We eat together and play too
We cheer each other up
We do everything together
We swim together, eat together, and even cry together
You're a true friend
We are best friends until the end
No matter what happens to us, we will always be friends

Grandpa
by Samantha Acker

Dear Grandpa
I know you're gone now
And all I can think is, "Wow"
I hardly knew you and that's okay
Because I'll see you again someday
You were too good to be true and so very fine
But I still can't believe that you were all mine
I didn't know you for very long
But I know your words like a peaceful song
I know you're out there
I know you're somewhere
I can sum it up for you in these very next words
I just wanted to tell you that ...
I love you!

Colors
by Abbey Bailey

Purple is ripe plum grapes
Purple is my warmest sweater
Purple is pretty lilacs
Purple is the ending sunset
Green is freshly cut grass
Green is the stems on every flower
Green is the luck of the Irish
Green is peas growing in a garden
Yellow is the rising sun
Yellow is sour lemons
Yellow is big tall sunflowers
Yellow is the mighty lion's mane
Blue is still water
Blue is the sky, with white clouds
Blue is swimming fish
Blue is the American flag
Colors are part of our life

The Gift
by Melanie Wizorek

I have always been the baby
But not anymore!
I can't wait to see that summer day
When Mom opens up the door
I will meet my little sibling
Who is adorable in every way
To see that baby smiling
Will brighten up my day
Staying up at night
Listening to it cry
Holding the baby tight
While watching the night fly
This baby is a gift
Sent from above
Who came to give us a lift
And someone else to love

Flowers Are Flowers
by Katelyn Valeski

Red flowers and pink flowers
Yellow flowers alike
What is the difference?
Flowers are flowers
And that is that
So why do they have names?
To me, flowers are flowers
And that is that

Evolution
by Nicole Critelli

Egg
White, hard
Warm, rough, fragile
Small, protective, tall, soft
Fuzzy, wet, feathery
Black, white
Penguin

Window
by Corrine Sharkey

See the world
Layers of thin ice
Inside-out mirror   rorrim tuo-edisni
Shelter, protector
What will occur when
Bro   ken?
                    May bite!
Don't touch!

Friend or enemy?

Meghan Hoerz

A sixth grade student,
Meghan is able to balance the demands of her many activities ...
volleyball, cheerleading, flute, and dance
with the necessary quiet time she needs to write.
It's easy to become excited about literature
when someone like Meghan does such a fantastic job
of showing how a good book
can unlock the door to a world of imagination.

Into the Pages
by Meghan Hoerz

"Come, come to me," the pages whisper in my ear
They pull me in like a bluebird singing its song
I want to be back in the quest
Sailing the pages of adventure
Hearing the thunderous laughter of triumph
As I conquer the tall cascading words
If I was let loose to venture its pages
There would be no saying when, or even if, I would be back
But for now I must lay down my head
The book shall remain a mystery till tomorrow night
As I drift asleep
The memories of my adventure will remain a secret

Marisia Hill

Marisia is a seventh grade student who loves to write,
and we find her work very intriguing.
Notice how in her poem, "Reflection"
she describes the faithfulness of her true love
not in summer, which is often the easiest season of togetherness,
but in the other three, where the measure of love is more demanding,
and therefore, shines that much brighter.

Reflection
by Marisia Hill

The cold breeze of winter hits my cheek
And there you are kissing me

In the fall, when leaves fall down on me
You are near

In the spring, when rain sprinkles across my arm
You are watching, and protecting me

I am thinking of you, and I show it by praying for you
Like I am right now

1st
Place

Max Wallack

As a student in the seventh grade,
Max has displayed great aptitude for creative writing.
His descriptive use of imagery is very effective,
as shown in his award winning poem, "Dementia"
in which he does an excellent job
of shedding a great deal of light
on an otherwise shadowy condition.
We would greatly look forward
to seeing more of Max's work.

Dementia
by Max Wallack

It gallops in silently on powerful hoofs
Snatching sweet, precious, forgotten memories
Turning true-blue loyal friends into treacherous strangers
Clogging synapses with emptiness
Crumbling trust into excruciating paranoia

With bleak darkness comes the anxious wakefulness of broad daylight
And bitter terror encompasses every living fiber
"If I sleep, where will I be when I wake up?"
The compulsion to run, the paralysis of fear

Mature, child-like dependence
Retracing youthful development, but in rapid reverse
Cureless medicines, meaningless conversations
Leading up to the inevitable

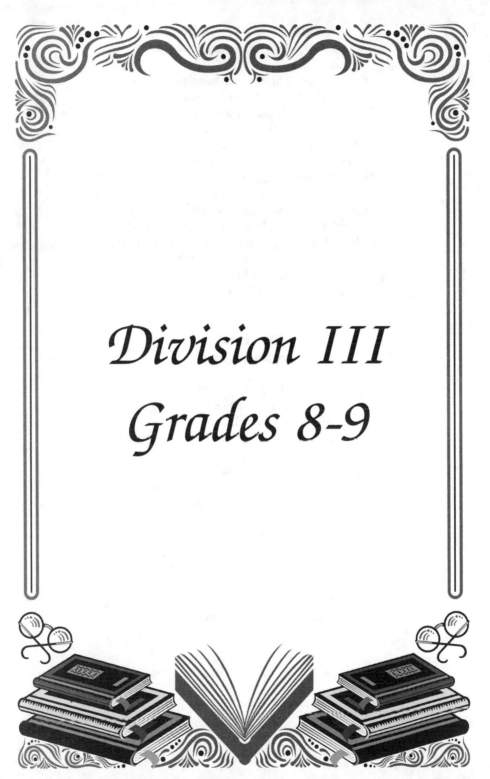

Division III
Grades 8-9

Chinese and French People
by Dillon Kline

One Chinese man had a pie
The other one only had one eye
One Chinese man had a bike
The other man had a trike
The other had five eyes, one man likes bats
The other man swims in a toxic waste vat
One French man had a snail
The other one had two nails
One Chinese man jumped over the Great Wall
Bang! The other Chinese man had a great fall
The last Chinese man was poor as a man that is poor
The last French man was colder than a door
The door loved bikes
The cat prefers a motorbike

My Goals
by James Rice

I want goals in my life
They keep me on track
And it's another challenge for me
My goals can even take years to accomplish
I want to be a good influence
I want to be a good leader
I want to skateboard as much as possible
Skateboarding is the best sport for me
Even though it costs a lot
It gives me a natural high
So I stay away from drugs like pot
Skateboarding is done in many places
Skateboarding is done by many races
Skateboarding is my favorite thing to do
Especially when I'm with my friends

Giovanni
by Bria Rishel

His eyes are as blue as the sky
His smile as bright as the sun
He is the apple of my eye
The one who brings all the fun
My love for him is like the ocean
My love for him, the never ending sky
My love for him a magic potion
My love is love that will never die
He is so kind and sweet
He sweeps me off my little feet
His voice, gentle and low
My love for him will still grow
He loves me every day
I still love him in every way!

Baseball
by Dylan Fox

Runners on, batters out
As the dedicated fans shout
The umpire squats down
This is the team, the town
Everyone on close vigilance
Hoping the ball clears the fence
Pitcher sweats, dugout watches
Waiting for the final stretch
Fans on their feet
Fans watching in the streets
Hoping for heroic actions
Listening for a solid connection
No exception
Of no perfection
Batter steps in the box
All eyes on him
The swing of the bat sends breezes of shocks
He will surely succeed
In the eyes of all who see

White Tigers
by Scott Folk

The tiger of fantasy
The tiger of dreams
This is where the tiger may roam free
No one to stop him
No one to get in his way
The white tiger as beautiful as it may be
But with a slash and growl he means, "Back away from me"
Have respect for these animals
As they might for you and me
Your dreams are like tigers, they take you anywhere
These are tigers of triumph, here to set your dreams free

Why?
by Alexis Bixler

I went to a party with a few of my friends
I had a few sodas and decided to dance
While dancing, the room became foggy
I had a stomachache and also a headache
My head as hot as a summer day
With a brick in my stomach, I headed for the doorway
My arms now the weight of a heavy bowling ball, it felt as if I could fall
I didn't understand what was going on, as I ran across the lawn
Getting into my car, I could barely see what was in front of me
Swerving all over the road, I felt like I was going to explode!
I suddenly flew forward, feeling cold cement all around me
I heard the sirens wailing
And hearing the paramedics saying, "She probably won't make it"
My breath getting short, knowing it's my last
Why did my friends have to do that? Putting drugs into my drink
Why couldn't this be them? I don't understand!
Please don't worry about me, I'll be in a better place
Looking down on you everyday, praying that you're okay
I still don't understand why this happened to me
Why did I ever have to go to that party?

In an Instant ...
by Paige Goss

Surrounded by darkness
A harsh world full of fright
A child dies of sorrow
Not a soul by their side
I reach out a hand and ask quietly ... why?
Who is to blame?
All that is left is a child ...
With no name
In an instant, one decision is made ...
The decision that stole a life of fame

Gypsy Rose
by Chelsea Kessler

I saw her in the paper, as beautiful as can be
When I looked into her eyes, she told me her story
"I've been abused and neglected
I need to find a home
Can you please help me find my way home?
I am as lost as a puppy
What do I do?
If you can love me, I can love you!"
Bam! It just hit me!
She needed my help
Home I must take her, home she must go!
Now she's a happy horse indeed!
Running, raging, laughing, have a good time
She is a hyper hippo all the time
To me right now, it's as if she grew legs!
She's my best friend and I wouldn't have it any other way!
Running through fields, getting in briars
Having lots of fun for hours and hours
I changed her life, it's great you see!
See what this horse has done to me!

Engine
by Calvin Nelson

I am sitting in the light brown leather seat
Silently listening to the beat
Rum, rum, rum, rum, rum
Goes the piston fleet
The pistons are like ill-treated steeds
Only paid by horse feed
My foot is the master
And gasoline is all the pistons need
Then the spark eats the pistons' food
Sending the pistons back down their giant metal tubes
The engine continues this with every piston
That is the sound to which I listen

Patches
by Shonna Wolfley

She runs through the house, all wild and crazy
Though most of the day she is lazy
Scratch!
The couch gets scratches
While she rolls on her patches
She sits in her chair
While she licks her hair
She snorts sometimes
So much to make me rhyme
She's as soft as a pillow
And makes the curtains willow
Her purr is a motor
It's usually quiet, but it lasts a while
She gets in trouble
Then makes it double
She flies through the air
And it makes us all stare
She can be loving
But she'd rather be running

No One
by Erica Bowling

No one knows how I feel inside
Everyday I just wanna run and hide
Crying myself to sleep at night
Will I ever see the light?
No one knows the real me
Open your eyes and maybe you'll see
The pain I feel, it's just not right
Hiding in the shadows throughout the night
No one knows where I hide my deepest scars
They're hidden behind iron bars
Love and hate, they're both the same
Both of them bring different kinds of pain
No one knows how I've lived my past
'Cause no one was there while it lasted
Dying inside and I don't know why
One day hoping to reach for the sky

The Big Game
by Zach Klingler

As we walk into the locker room
All as one team
It's as silent as the sleeping moon
We can and will play like a machine
Then they ask if I saw the letter
I then read the note
It will make me play better
I was as mad as a slapped bull
Crash, bang, boom!
Tackle after tackle
Yard after yard
As we go down the field
The other team is in team yield
I am proud to be the captain of this!

Soccer Players
by Chris Trawitz

Playing soccer is like riding a bike for the first time
You have fun and accomplished a task
The ball is a human, it runs down the field
Soccer soothes several situations
Attack the ball!
Do not fall
Set the ball
Shoot the ball
We'll have fun all and all!
It is a fun game and teamworking game
Like they say, "There is no I in team"
But when you win a game then yell, hear us shouting!
That is the game of soccer
'Sloosh' goes the soccer ball to the back of the net!

Ballbreaker
by Brandon Katherman

AC/DC rocks
Angus Young is the lead guitarist
He rocks
He can run while playing the guitar
Brian Johnson is the vocals
They are like the best band
Thunderstruck, bam!
They still stand!

Rain
by Gabrielle Pitts

As I sit and watch the rain
Drip, drip, drip, from above
Like the birds chirping away
I get a feeling, a feeling that will never go away
That will hunt me day and night
As I sit and watch the rain come down
Like water balloons ready to burst open with a splash
I get that feeling, the feeling that needs to be alone
The feeling that's a secret and will never be shown

Heroes of September 11, 2001
by Cammeron Ogden

There's a hero in all of us, someone once said
But no one knew it was true until that day of dread
There's a hero in the woman who was sitting at her desk
Going about her "normal day", unsure of what would happen next
There's a hero in every policeman, carrying out his duties as assigned
Only to die a hero's death with his brothers, side by side
There's a hero in every firefighter, who fought that awful blaze
Knowing, as they pulled burning bodies, today may be one of their last days
There's a hero in every passenger, in every car
Bravely going about their day, they're heroes from afar
There's a hero in every child, who lost a parent that day
Every tear they cried would symbolize how much they wish they could say
There's a hero in every baby born, bringing life to the world
Proving, in a time of tragedy, miracles can unfurl
There's a hero in every parent, who looked at their child to explain
What is this world coming to? America shall never be the same
There's a hero in all of us, someone once said
Now everyone knows that it is true, because of that day of dread

Time
by Jacob Coomes

Time is something you cannot change
It's as complicated as unscrambling an egg
If you try, you can only scream and beg
Time is something you cannot change
Think about your presents opening with a rip last December
They're just memories that cannot be rearranged
You can't relive them, you can only remember
Time is something you cannot change
As time pushes you forward, you look back at what you have done
That's when you realize you have to forget the past
And look at what is right in front of you, which is that morning sun
Time is something you cannot change

Attitude
by McKenzie Moore

Attitude is everything
Helps you stay alive
Attitude is everything
But only the strong survive
Attitude is everything
Will you ever grow?
Attitude is everything
Will anyone ever know?
Attitude is everything
Proving all your strengths
Attitude is everything
Reaching for great lengths
Attitude is everything
Takes you to amazing heights
Attitude is everything
Forces you to win your fight
Attitude is everything
But only the strong survive
Attitude is everything
Will you stay alive?

Friend
by Crystal Rodrigues

Jenlisa is Monet
Her drawing skills are amazing
Jenlisa is a monkey
How she plays–it's crazy
Jenlisa is a high-bounce ball
Bouncing off the roof–how she runs
Jenlisa is like a kangaroo
Jumping all over the place–how high she jumps
Jenlisa is a clown
How she makes people smile

St. Nick
by Tylor O'Connell

Oh my, it is jolly St. Nick
Look at his belly, so big and thick
Look at him leave gifts under my tree
Look at him laugh and shake his belly with glee
In excitement he left so fast
Oh my, look what house he did pass
The house of Von Geis
Where everyone was nice
So he had to go back
For his Christmas snack

In the Darkness: A Symbol of Death
by C.F. Howsy III

You see the black velvet coming
Legs heavy, you start running
What lurks within has opened an eye
A red and bloody eye
It reaches out
You don't shout
It grabs you tightly around the waist
Your worst fear is yet to be faced
It looks up and down you
A mouth opens and swallows you
As you fall through its nasty depths
You fall, stand up, and take some steps
Down you fall again with a scream
You wake up, it's all been a dream
You turn around, there the darkness is
He swallows you with an evil hiss
You lie there while no eyes blink
You're dead, you never would think

Dreaming
by Zachary Raker

A five-year old dreaming of becoming a pro
Learning the sport and learning to throw
A twelve-year old dreaming of becoming a pro
Loving the sport and beginning to grow
Ten years later he is now a pro
He is the best
But he wants to go
Back to the nest

To Speak In English Good
by Nancy Dennehy

Why can't I speak in English good?
In school, they learned me that I could
Learn new things that I ain't knowed
And read 'bout things that I been showed
So hear me, younguns, what I says
Hear me, childs and gals and mens
Mind your teachers as you should
So you can speak in English good

Lovely Fall
by Daisy Keiser

Outside your house the wind whistles
The trees blow back and forth
It's starting to get cold as an icebox
When the trees start to lose their leaves
You see them spread all over the ground
Colors of green and red and orange
The air smells fresh and clean
You hear the squeaky brakes from the bus as the kids go back to school
The leaves crunching as the kids run through their yards

Running
by Sarah Thomas

You start at a slow jog
But suddenly
A jolt of energy
Runs through you
Like a shock wave
Your legs start
Flying ...
And your heart screams
Faster, faster, faster
And before you know it
You're soaring
No one can touch you
You're invincible
You're rising up ...
A balloon
Rising, rising ...
To a place
That no one
Has ever been
Before ..

Box of Crayons
by Megan Koontz

Life can be a box of crayons
Full of bright and dull colors
The good things are bright
And full of passion
And dreams you never thought could exist
The dull colors represent
The pain and heartache of depression
Life hands you this big box of crayons
Drawing the masterpiece of your life
Each dream that happens
Adds another dull color, comes into view
But when your masterpiece is finished
So is your life

My Mind
by Chelsie Norris

I've been someone else for so long, I can't see where I've gone
I've lied about this, done that, hung out with the wrong cat, and got scratched
Been in and out of trouble so much, it all feels fake to the touch
I've seen stuff that most people would stop and say, "Enough"
But I kept on going and now I'm not slowing
I'm in this creek too deep, but I've got to keep rowing
I see no changes, that's why I fill these pages everyday
I go through stages to prove myself, to let me know that I can go the distance
It's like every time I blink, I miss the important stuff
I'm supposed to see, but it's like my mind stays clear
Like I'm supposed to do something with my life
But when I close my eyes, I see nothing in my head
I look back at all my dead friends and sometimes I think this is the end
But then something runs through my head saying
"I'm not meant to be dead, not yet, I need to make it"
This is me, there is no way I could fake it, for the ones who wonder what I think
This is just a piece of my mind
I'll write the rest when it's my time

Just Her Memories
by Eleanor Foltz

As I look upon her face
I can see her laugh
I can see her cry
I can see her smile …
Oh, how I miss her so with every tear I cry
I can see her in my eyes, in my memories, in my painful dreams …
Oh, how much pain she puts me through just with her memories
Every moment that passes, I lose more of myself
Just to keep her close to me, it's nothing but her memory
Every painful memory
Every living day
Every passing moment
Every time I cry …
I see her in my dreams; it's nothing but her memories
That's my little girl, my sister, my friend, my family
I miss you
I love you
My memory

Cow Tipping
by Julia Welding

Tip or toe, the cows all go
Down onto the ground
The farmer comes with his gun
And then releases the hound
Black and white all through the night
When all you hear is moos
You wish to yourself that you'd have brought
Some better running shoes
I drop and fall
And try to crawl
To escape from the dog
But man, was it really hard because of all the fog
Then I stood up and then went home
To ask Mom what was for dinner
To my surprise, before my eyes
She fed me some cow liver

Pray For Pap
by Sarah Jacobs

Pap has an illness
It's getting hard to deal with
You think it's gonna get better
Because Pap isn't a quitter
But it's getting worse
Pretty soon we are gonna have to call the nurse
Pray that he doesn't need a hearse
Pray for Pap
It's the best thing to do
He is going to get strong
And make it through
But only with the help from you
Pray for Pap
It's the best thing you can do

Summary
Summer
by Nick Ravida

I can't wait till summer
All of the sunny days, wearing shorts
Tons of people playing down at the courts
Winter is a real bummer
I love the long nights playing release
We won't need anymore fleece
It starts to get dark around nine
All the honeys in bikinis looking fine
All of the school kids reuniting
Hopefully there will be no fighting
Beautiful day for golfing on green grass
Fishing in the streams and catching huge bass
I can't wait till summer

Dreams ...
by Anthony Sorrentino

When you get in your bed
And the sheep start leaping
You lay down your head
And you start sleeping
You start to think magnificent dreams
Sometimes you're happy
Sometimes you scream
You can even enter with a clown named Slappy
You have no regrets
You feel no sorrow
So enjoy yourself
Until tomorrow ...

Forgotten
by Juile Shipley

Forget his name
Forget his smile
Forget the love you once had
Remember, he is long gone
Forget the memories
Forget the day you met him
Remember, he's forgotten you

Wishing
by Helen Kim

The red balloon
Longs to float up
To touch the sky
To leave everyone behind
As it climbs up and up
Instead, it is held down
Trapped in the tiny hands
Of a little birthday boy
Who just won't let it go

The American Dream
by Alex Mykeloff

Power, wealth, and greed
All these things you just don't need
For you see
It's not all it's cracked up to be
You're not liked for you
People think you're snobby too
And money, the root of all evil
Turns you into the biggest weasel
So if there is one thing that I deemed
Love is all you need for the American Dream

A Walk In the Woods
by Bryce Johnson

As we walk we can hear
The leaves crunching under our feet
The trees are singing
As the wispy wind blows through their arms
The crows are like
Children screaming as they fly overhead
The squirrels fighting in the
Trees like an old married couple
The clouds dancing as if they are on fire
The honey bees are deafening
The smell of honeysuckle is amazing
The great outdoors is an endless adventure!

Dreams
by Alex Hogan

A dream is a window to your thoughts or wishes
A dream can become a new world that mocks reality
But when one comes to think a dream is real
They may just find it has lethality
Surely you may fly upon a winged horse's back
But will you remember to look back
To your family, friends and passions
Who are always there, love, accepting?
A dream can give you better things, bigger things, brighter things
Things you don't need, but in utter greed
You may just find your longing true
But this should not strike a blow to you
For human nature contains greed, but if in a dream
It causes no harm, no splits at the seam
But even in flaw, a dream is a miracle
A pinnacle of light in the dark
So in the end of a dream or story
One is filled with illusory glory
But a happiness that does not depart
From the depths of the heart

The Hurricane
by John Collins

I heard the wind howling in the night
I saw the wind rustle the leaves
Like a funnel from the sky
I saw the waves smack the rocks
Like a car crash on the highway
The lightning bolts struck the earth
As if they were mad
I felt the rain pelt my skin
Like a whip cracking at my spine
You may ask what storm is so violent
I call it a hurricane

The Love of Music
by Katelyn Waltimyer

Ah, music!
The sweet melody flowing from my fingers
The glorious, ringing tones escaping through my lips
Bursting with the excitement
Of sharing the gift with the world
Through the ages, music has been the saving grace
Of many a poor and desperate soul
But the brilliant minds that produce the gift understand
Its true purpose is not to entertain the artist
But to touch the hearts of those who listen

Guilt
by Sunshine Colvin

A silent reminder of our past
Of our misdeeds
Of our failures
A lurking sea of darkness
Waiting in the very corners of our minds
Watching to see if our guards drop
And when they do
It's ready
Ready to creep up behind us
Ready, at any moment, to suffocate us with its moonless night
It's something we desperately try to run from
But we all know it's fruitless
A waste of time
Because eventually it finds you
And then it consumes you

Dealing With a Loss
by Brittany Kemp

Weeping
Tears rolling down like a steady stream
I see no end to this moment of sorrow
Friends, family are trying to comfort me with calm, soothing words
Some try to hold me close
"Shh! Shh! Shh!" they whisper in my ear
But nothing soothes the sharp pain that trudges on
My eyes are puffy, red cherries
That look as though they are about to burst
I lie in bed
Night drawing close, a blanket of darkness
My head lays on my pillow
Eyes drooping, longing for sleep
I drift into a deep sleep

Off To the Side
by Casey Dimoff

Off to the side in deep seclusion
I sit and watch what I wish I were doing
I cannot speak or make a noise
This was supposed to be a great joy
I envy the others, the trust they have gained
As I sit and watch, severely pained
There's nothing I can do, that I must accept
As they have done all one can expect
Their egos get bigger with every praise and shout
I feel like to nothing I'll ever amount
I surpass them in many other things
However, they can all crush me in the ring
Their smiles gleam bright like stars in the sky
As I sit and watch, I almost cry
They think they're good to such great length
I'm not given a chance to show my strength
So off to the side in deep seclusion
I sit and watch what I wish I were doing

Her Face
by Taylor Flinchbaugh

Her face is white as snow
With makeup to give it color
But I know it's all fake
Her hair wasn't this curly
The curls just weren't that small
They were bigger and looser
Don't they know anything?
I want to yell at them
They didn't do it right
My great-grandmother didn't look like that
Are you kidding me?
You call yourselves professionals
But you just made it worse
I could have done a better job myself
I loved her so much
And I still visit her grave
But when I remember her
I remember what they did to her face

Food
by Shane Wantz

The smell in the air, on a bright sunny day
I can't see it from so far away
I go for a walk, then see it right now
Somebody said, "Are you cooking a cow?"
I thought it was chicken, but I guess it is not
As long as it's not cooked in a pot
The burger was cooking on top of the grill
Everyone there was having a thrill
The burgers sizzled like bacon in a pan
The temperature was hot, so I needed a fan
The burgers were done, now it's time to have the real fun
The flame was as bright as the sun, everyone was using a bun
I take the first bite, it is really good
It tastes better than I thought it would
The burgers tasted as good as pie
Now it's time to say good-bye

Football
by Josh Andrezywski

Swish! Football tearing through the air
The clock keeps clicking down
Grrr! Men lined up pair by pair
We're gonna win no doubt
It's fourth down and it's time to go
Just one yard left to make
It's time to show them who's the pro
We're here with all at stake
I run and try to make it in
So close we have to have it
But now I'm found in a four man pin
Last thing I know, I'm getting hit
Rushed off the field, covered in dirt
Coach just looks and smiles
I made it in, even though I'm hurt
Feel like I ran for miles
I did it and it feels so good
I already feel the fame
I didn't really think I could
I'm the champion of the game

Memories of a Friendship
by Brandon Delp

Nathan and I played for hours on end
Waiting for my grandma to call us both in
She made spaghetti for lunch
Our favorite, we had a brunch
Next, we had to take a nap
When we woke, we met down back Pap
He gave us cookies and we sat on his lap
Then he gave us jobs to pick up walnuts out back
Thud is what we heard as the walnuts spit black
As we sit down, we hear a boom in the sky
We both know it is soon time
When we hear the rain splat as it flies by
Night comes so soon
Then out creeps the moon
Wishing us both a good night

The Light From the Darkness
by Darien Seiple

I come home from school crying, I grab the blade from the drawer
I hold it thinking, what would my life be like if I were happy?
I hold it to my wrist, I press real hard
I slide it across my pale arm, as my arm bleeds and cries out crimson blood
As I sit on the floor in front of the white and red door
I said to myself, this is life, this is life and I've wasted it
Wasted it being paranoid about people and what they think
Worrying about what I look like
A short while after, my hands and feet get cold and numb
The floor is hard and cold like the harsh cold night
I set the blade to my skin once again
But I stop and think before I slide it across my skin
I think to myself, I'm dying, I'm killing myself, day by day
These scars are bad memories I cannot take
I try to erase them, but they are burned into my mind, permanently there
I've shut myself out, letting people get under my skin
At that thought, a woman dressed beautifully in white appeared
And walked towards me
I then realized, she is the one, my bleeding stopped instantly
I thought she was the angel of death coming to take me to a better place
The love she has shown me is unreal and can't be put into words
All I can say is she's the one, she came and stayed with me through the rough times
Ever since that day there's been life in my life
She has shown me the good things in life
The things to live and die for, but the best thing of all to chase for in life is ... Love

Tragic Magic
by Uriah Graham

Buzzing cheeks and brain desolation
Warm feet and burning exhalation
Heightened senses, yet the nervous system is shut down
Show the fences, flash smiles, and frowns
Tranquility with wobbly knees
Harmony against enemies
Glazed windows with a drooping noise escape
Light bathed meadows that will later prove to be fake
A great deal of melancholy and stress is now gone
But I failed the test and am now a pawn

The Songbirds and the Lilies
by Blake Cutshall

The songbirds and the lilies
Are taken care of
They merely rest in the field
Or sing on a branch
Beautiful for all to see
While human hands work
Fingernails, dirt underneath
The people have to hurt
Why can't I be a lily
Or a songbird?
For they live happy and free
Lord, am I not worth much more
In your eyes than these?
Oh, my Lord above
Will you not take care of me?

The Summer of Dreams
by Melissa Cox

Every shining summer day
I love to go outside and play
I rustle through brush and jump through leaves
Sometimes I even crawl on my knees
In the morning I wake up
I jump out of bed almost knocking the clock
I yawn and stretch and dip very low
While the sun shines at full glow
I fly down the steps, almost falling with excitement
For today is the day I get to go hiking
I gush down my pancakes and swoosh down my milk
My hiking stick is even covered with silk
All through the day I spin and fly
I wish some day I could be free in the sky
I flop in the grass and lay flat on my back
I surely don't know when I will ever be back
While I lay here, I sit and I think
I think of the breeze and the wind and the trees
I think of my future and what is in store
I believe in this dream and how astounding I'll be

The Slave's Thoughts!
by Brittany White

As I stare into the body of water
I see a body in the water
My reflection is a shocking sight
Scars, gashes, and deformed fingers; I see ribs
I can feel the pain and torture of what has happened to me
But this is my burden to bear
Knowing that blacks die from here to there
We shall be free in one thought or another
But now, it's not only my burden to bear
All blacks bear the pain with me
Because we fight, we run; the whites beat us
Not a single thought in my head but to be free

Oh, How I Hate Thee
by Emily Smeltzer

When you came into my life
I thought it was the greatest
But once I got to know you
Oh, how I despise you so
Work harder, harder is all I ever hear you say
Every day it starts with good morning, now comes the fun
Hours and hours of sweat and burn
If something's not right, you respond
With hatred until I can learn
Criticize you must, for I know why
You are afraid of what might become
Of our lives
You insist it's for the best
But you only care about yourself
Finally it's over, it has ended
The last words you say mean nothing to me
It is the last time I will ever face you again
But you do not know what is to come
All you can say is "Good night, Champion"
My pain has finally ended

In the Morning ...
by Ashley Cox

In the morning I walk outside
I see grass glistening its watery wings
The air seems fresh and my cares flow away
I look at the ocean and see the bay
The trees stand tall with a new day ahead
Their strength renewed with a night full of rest
The branches are stretching out to me with life
I see their leaves bursting with green life
The ocean to my left, the woods to my right
I choose to walk on the sand-covered ground, where crabs crawl in holes
With waves roaring and seagulls soaring, why would you let this day go?
The sun is bright, I see to my right
The wonders of life in the palm of God's hand
Seashells are beautifully crafted by the sea, all part of this glorious plan
I lay on the ground with my back on the sand
I see the sky with its millions of wonders
The clouds soar above me and I lie and stare
The beach is magnificent, so I tend to stay there to think
Time flies before your eyes and this place makes it feel like time stops
As quick as you know it, everything can go away as fast as a blink

Painting
by Shannon Green

Brush in my hand, flowering free like a bird
Speaking through pictures instead of through words
My palette is filled with contrasting hues
From the lightest of pinks to the darkest of blues
An easel holding a canvas so blank and white
Is about to be filled with colors so bright
A scene of the park with a cloudy blue sky
Some birds soaring towards the sun way up high
The final result hangs on the wall
A source of delight to one and to all

Space Is a Mysterious Place
by Krista Sadecky

As the sun goes down
The moon shines bright
All the stars
Come out at night!
Some comets shoot across the sky
And as you look up, you from Earth
You wonder
How and why?
All eight planets
Moving in their orbits
Are whirling and speeding around the sun
Alas, their race is never done!
Further off we shall go
To where the stardust puts on a show
Light-years and light-years away
Even past our Milky Way
You have to wonder
Will the planets always align
Or will they someday
Stop on a dime?
Black holes, a glitch in space
They are awesome yet scary
What do they mean for our human race?
Space is a mysterious place

Memory
by Kyle O'Loughlin

Playing outside in spring, enjoying all the sports
Enjoying every second with friends
Playing by the pool in the cool water
Playing basketball, watching the ball swoosh
Playing baseball, crushing it far
Running to catch it, and getting the out
Camping in the woods, setting up the tents
Fishing in the river, catching all the fish
Lighting a fire, and telling stories

For Me
by Tonya Tucker

For me the Holocaust is a prime example of the future not being bright
So many people's souls had no light
They had no dreams, no hopes, or joys
None of the little children had toys
All they had was a shovel and dirt
To cover up all of their hurt
Women, children, and men all separated
Thank God none decapitated
But even worse, they watched their loved ones die
Horrible deaths started by one lie
By Hitler
But then when all hope is lost
Hope rescues and all are free
But those whose lives are lost can never leave

Stranger On the Train
by Marisa Quiery

Predictable, same seat
Stranger on the train
Always looking sad, as if he doesn't know how to smile
As if he hadn't talked to anyone for awhile
He gazes out the window, looking at the blurred trees
As I look, I wonder, why is he so sad?
Stranger on the train
I board the train after him and get off sooner
I long to meet this stranger on the train
Does this stranger see me?
Does he, too, wonder about me?
We often have awkward eye contact
He looks at me, quickly away
I stand up ... "Hello stranger on the train"

Sleep
by Jordan Waddell

Sleeping is good
It's all warm and bubbly
The covers protect me
It always refreshes me
Never get enough, you never can 'cause
Every time you wake up, you go back again
You can sleep on your back, on your side
On your belly, heck, even upside down
You can sleep in a tent, on a boat
In the car, in the rain
On a train , in a plane
You can sleep outside on the porch
Or inside on the couch
No matter what, sleep is always good
You can sleep with a friend, or by yourself
No matter what, you will be refreshed
You can have many dreams or none at all
You can wake up, and say bye for now
But guess what?
That was just a dream!

Stupid Little Love Poem
by Emily Faro

Okay, so let's get started, you know just how it goes
It's just another one of those cheesy love poems
You know the one I'm talking about, oh yes you do
The one that spills my heart and soul and guts all to you
The one that says "I love you" in every single line
The one that says you will love me too, if I just give you time
Because we're simple girls you know, we live our lives day to day
Thinking of that one special guy who will never go away
We draw those little hearts in every notebook we can find
We scribble your name in bubble letters, just to pass the time
And even though half the time, you probably don't even care
We still do those little things, like laugh and twist our hair
Because we're just simple girls now, we live our lives day to day
Living on those love poems, and every word you say

Mother's Day, 2007
by Victoria Gibson

You do so much for me
When I grow up, you're everything I want to be
You're a better mother than the rest
Let's just say you are the best
You're as beautiful and bright as the morning sun
You are also very, very fun
Let's just say I love you so
You're cooler than anyone I know
You're too good for words to say
Other than saying, "Happy Mother's Day"

My Flower
by Lauryn Eggen

It started with a glance
That's all, just a glance
It ended with a death
A horrible, tragic death
He saw me, I saw him
He walks over, talks to me
Talks to me like a real person
With him, I'm not the lonely girl
With him, I mean the world to him
And gradually we grow
The friendship seed is planted
Blooming into love
Then the hailstorm, the drunk driver
Shatters our love
We had fought, he drove home
10 minutes later and I'd still be whole
I'm torn, never to be one again
That's why it doesn't end with one death
It ends with two

Mountaintops
by Shawn Gannon

Perched high upon my mountaintop
Peering down at all that encompasses my domain
Elevated from the rest
Put on a pedestal for all to see
I look back on simpler times
Whence my companions and I scaled mountains together
But they slowed as the elevation rose
And I continued, my ambition driving me
Oblivious to the others falling back beneath the clouds
As I reached the summit and looked around
No one was left to share my joy
Losing perspective of what was important
I now retire to the solitude of my sky-bound perch
Gazing into the warmth of the dawning sun
I envision other mountaintops in the distance
And upon them I recognize my companions
Singing and rejoicing that the new day has come
Seeing my companions so content on their Elysian crest
I reflect in the silence of my mountaintop

Space
by Anthony Grazioso

I am space
Awe inspiring
Mind boggling
Thought creating
Constellation creating
Planet revolving
Stars imploding
Black hole forming
NASA studying
Mission launching
Satellite flashing
Frequency broadcasting
Scientist confusing
Book writing
Ego humbling
I am infinity

My Sick Grandma
by Joseph Nelson

I am very sad now
Throughout my years
But before I wasn't
My grandma is sick
Which is not cool for me
I am very sad now
That my grandma is sick
She is going through chemo
All because of smoking
I am very sad now
She is not herself these days
She is skinny and in pain
She is losing her hair
I am very sad now
I love and look after her
But now she is gonna die
Sooner than later
I am very sad now
But before I wasn't
My grandma is sick

Are You Here?
by Heather Van Overschelde

Are you here?
In the dark where I am scared
To hold and comfort me
Are you here?
In this lonely world
Where I have no one to make me feel special
Are you here?
In the wind
I can feel and hear you
But I cannot see you
You are not here?
But I will wait for you
Until we meet again
I love you, Grandpa

The Four Seasons
by Daniel Bechen

Spring
Calm and wet
Spring
New and unfamiliar
Summer
Blistery and dry
Summer
Hard and fun
Fall
Colorful and cool
Fall
Peaceful and fun
Winter
Cold and frozen
Winter
White and fluffy

Ten Things I Hate About You
by Cassidy Wormstadt

I hate that you think you're all that
I hate that you think everyone adores you
I hate that you think you're so hot
I hate the way you dress
I hate that you think you're so smart
I hate that you take all of the credit
I hate that you talk about me behind my back
I hate that you think you're the greatest singer in the world
I hate that you are mean to everyone
But most of all I hate how I thought we were friends

No Emotion
by Brittany Birgfeld

Eyes glazed over
Crooked smile on your face
Stare them down
Whatever it takes
Show them no emotion
Show them no pain
Show them what it takes
To live a life full of pain
Show them what they did to you
No emotion on your face
Lost your sense of happiness
Taken away by this disgrace

I Sleep, I Dream, I Awake
by Cheryl Clish

As the sun sets and darkness appears
I hear wind christening the leaves as they dream to sleep
Flowers close up for another day with a song of a bird
Stars give a night light to glistening streams, to ripple of sound
Beyond is a much more magical feeling
Looking up, you see a star of light
It dances with you and shows nature around you
It is a beautiful night of dark
Too beautiful to paint
Too beautiful to disturb
The feeling of the warm breeze hugs me as I sleep
I hear the wind whistling in my ear
A nightmare haunts me in my storm
I feel threatened to ride it out
The stars cling to night fall
The morning is upon the dew of wetness to start a new day
As the star kissed night crosses with sound of change
Light appears again with the scene disappearing out of blank dark
As the sun comes up, you see two butterflies dancing along the bed of flowers
They are anxious to be alive and to live another day from peace of the night
As I awake, it appears to me to be a lively world outside of darkness
But still beautiful from the inside out

Your Girl
by Tenesa Deutz

I was your strawberry girl
The girl who would snarf down a pound of strawberries with you for a snack
Then clean out the rest of them for dinner
Enveloped in heavy cream
I was your cowgirl
The girl who would throw on a cowboy hat
Grab your hand and ask
"When can we ride the horses?"
I was your sale barn girl
The girl who told you what horse was best for riding
And which calf was the cutest
I also knew exactly how to twist your arm
To receive a Tootsie Roll Pop from the auctioneer
I was your grand girl
The girl who was happy to be held by you when I was born
The girl who cried at your funeral when you died
You were my grandpa
I was your girl
Grandpa, you will be missed and loved forever

Dear God
by Nicole Link

Dear God,
Today I helped a person
It made me feel good
He looked at me and looked unsure
I guided him across the street
And to his red brick house
He thanked me and asked if I could stay a while
He told me about all of his life
And about his family
They all had died in an accident
He said he had been alone for many years
I said, "Well, you're not alone anymore"
I saw a tear run down his face
He said thank you and looked happy
Serving others is like serving God
He is never alone anymore, because God led me to him

Time
by Rebecca Force

Time can end
And yet it can not
Like existence
You can die and be gone
But you are never truly gone
Your memory lives on
But how can it end?
Time is endless
Yet everything must end
How will we know when time is gone?
No one will
Once time stops
Everything must stop
Everything must die
Everything must disappear
Into the nothingness of time

Love
by Jonathan David

It's harder than it seems
But when it's true it gleams
When you have it, you can't hide it
A couple stands beside it
It can sting like a dart
Or fill up your heart
You should have it when you marry
And you hope that it will carry
Throughout the ages, it's clear
Love is always near

True Friend
by Destiny Luckenbaugh

Always there
When I need you
Always listening
And caring carefully
About my problems
As if they were your own
Always there to comfort me
And softly dry my tears
As if I were you little sister
Making time for me
Even when you are busy
Ha, ha, ha
We always laugh together
You are a good friend
You are a true friend

School Ain't Cool
by Ned Einsig III

When we come to school in the morning
It is so boring
All the kids are snoring
School ain't cool
It makes me wanna drool
All the teachers enforce their evil rule
I'd rather be at the pool
School is lame
It was since the moment I came
Every year is the same
The teachers play their evil game
The Language Arts teacher always got an evil smile
The Science teacher's a crocodile
School's goin' out of style
The Math teacher's always drinkin' beer
The History teacher's as old as Paul Revere

What Is My Name?
by Ariana Zak

I am something most people know
Whether I come from friends or family
Mothers use me to soothe a child's tears
What am I?
I can rain down like bubbles, pop
Or just hang around in the air
Almost everyone knows about me
So, what is my name?
I have a special holiday
But I'm used throughout the year
When people don't show me to their families
It makes me shed a tear
What is my name?
What am I?
And if you haven't guessed yet
My name has four letters
And hate is my foe
Now do you know
What am I?

The Only Difference
by Alexis Stough

You're hurting your family and losing your friends
The pain you cause loved ones isn't worth it in the end
You're disgusting to look at and awful to smell
Your heart's getting weaker as your lungs cry out for help
That awful addiction that you hold in your fingers
Is impossible to run away from when your longing for it lingers
The smoke in your throat is the death warrant you demanded
The life you once lived, you've completely abandoned
You'd die for another, an escape from the stress
The only difference between smoking and suicide, is the coverage of the press

Iwo Jima
by Bryce Fuchs

Near the ground at Sulfur Island
My feet met the pungent Earth
The zing of mortars everywhere
Trying to kill us
It seemed to never stop
Then we knew it was a running war

My Pap
by Briana Boyer

The sun is out
The leaves are scattering
A perfect day turned around
He has won the race
He will feel no more pain
When they tell me
I'm turned around
Its name is cancer
That took my pap's life
He is in Heaven
I will always remember you ...
I love you

Ache
by Danielle Myers

His hair is pink
He's so dumb that he's hanging upside down on a monkey bar
He looks so funny
Ouch!
He just took a hit to his head
One of his friends just ran into him
Now he has a big ache in his head
Easy to think he wasn't very happy about this ache
That he now has to suffer with this ache for the rest of the day
I feel so bad for him
I should have stood in front of him to prevent it
Then he wouldn't have this ache

Before
by Griffith Gentilcore

Before technology
Before building
Before video games
Before television
Before cities
Before states
Before countries
Before religion
Before woman
Before man
Before the Jurassic period
Before seven hundred million years ago
Before the earth
Before the sun
Before the moon
Before the systems
Before galaxies
Before finding something
There was nothing

Sunshine
by Heaven Kershaw

You are my sunshine on a cloudy day
The flower that brightens my spirits in every way
The strength I need when I am weak
When my world seems so very bleak
When everything is black as coal
When everything is gone
I know that you will be there with open arms
You are my rainbow on a rainy day
The arms that support me in various ways
You're the light that keeps me going
Looking for the end of the tunnel that's finally showing
You are my sunshine
Whose beauty can blind
No matter how distinctively kind

Just One
by Elena Leib

Just one glance, you can tell so much
Mad or happy, sad or snappy
Just one glance and your world stops ...
Dead in its tracks
And it all becomes clear
The clutter erased
And the true meaning escapes
Just one glance, and a window opens
A window opens to a whole new world
Just one glance and a stranger becomes a friend
In a moment of doubt
But you didn't miss out
Now the clutter's crased
And the true meaning's escaped
Just one glance, straight in the eye
Mad or happy, sad or snappy
Just one smile to help you get by
And a stranger becomes a friend

The Lake
by Tyler Smith

The lake
A place of peace and beauty
Untouched by technology
Where fishermen cast out their lines
And osprey and eagles circle
Around unsuspecting fish
Where ducks swim with their young
And pike patrol the waters for a snack
And when the sun sets
The Earth is covered with a blanket
Of red, yellow, blues, and oranges
And a chorus of loons joins to sing nature's song
The lake

Listen .Closely
by Carly Higgins

A bird calls and a cricket chirps
As the wind blows
And a bee buzzes a busy melody
This is the sound of nature's song
The water flows
A frog croaks
A cat purrs
A fish jumps
The mirrored surface of the pond breaks
The weeds rustle
A dog barks
And a young girl, writing, stirs
Clouds gather and rain begins to fall
And the girl hides under the trees
She sits there and listens to nature's beautiful song
The rain stops
The young girl emerges and claps as the trees bow
Everything falls silent as the song ends
When it starts again you may hear it as well
But only if you listen closely

Ode To 39
by Matt Mahan

It's first and goal, game's on the line, the sky was getting darker
Coach Tomlin simply would not resign, 'cause he had Willie Parker
Ten seconds left, ball's on the three
The play: a run to the right, the opposing team was filled with glee
They thought they won the fight, the ball is snapped, the crowd is still
As Willie takes the ball, Tomlin's thinking, "What a thrill!"
This is better than the mall!
Parker goes right, then straight to the goal
Fast Willie crossed the line
The Steelers have won the Super Bowl, because of 39

Another Day On the Farm
by Richard Pritts

Silver towers swallow up seas of gold
As keys bring pistons up to speed
Just another day on the farm
The barn is being filled with bales of gold
A large tin cage holds the precious cobs
The deer are in the fields eating what is left
Just another day on the farm
A boy and his dog check the fence
While a hunter hopes for a deer to jump out of the fields
The autumn leaves form a tornado
I lace up my boots and go to the barn
There are all my friends staring intently
I water, feed, and apportion hay
Finally, the end of the day

To My Dad
by Caitlynn Houk

When I was young you were always there to hold my hand and say, "I care"
Encourage me along the way, along each step a different day
Laugh a heck of a lot and say don't ever smoke pot
You teach me how to do only good things in life
And to never judge and only do what is right
My dad's hands are never clean although he is a working man
He is never that mean
He cracks half a smile only once in a while
Doesn't like to show his teeth unless they are shiny, polished, and in style
My dad is the kind of man that performs the unexplainable
People usually stare, but my dad says that doesn't bother me because I don't care
There are characteristics in every person that brings out your smile
Therefore my dad has too many and I will love him for quite a while

Rivers
by Caitlin Gleason

Of all in nature, large and small
I envy rivers most of all
When stones and boats have come and gone
They stay the course and carry on
They hug the land with easy glide
And meet the ocean, arms open wide
They can't be troubled with clouds of grey
For soon arrives the light of day
Please excuse this foolish drawl
But more than things that walk or crawl
I envy rivers most of all

Inside of Me
by Nikki McLaughlin

To see the world through my eyes
You'd have to wipe away the tears I cry
Uncover the secrets I once buried
Lift the weight off my shoulders I must carry
Find the real me inside with all this pain
Describe the things I just can't explain
Pick up the pieces of my broken heart
Solve the mystery of what made my world fall apart
Fill the emptiness that comes from within
Discover the things that make my head spin
Expose the true feelings I have for him
Force away all the pressure to make me too slim
Determine my need for freedom and space
This is my life, my world to embrace
If you endure all the obstacles in my world
You'll realize that I'm just your average girl
My hopes and dreams are all part of me
And when the time comes, I'll let them be free

Single Moment
by Deanna Nagle

One minute I'm sitting in my room
Next: I'm lying face down on my bedroom floor
Watching myself from above … wondering
What's going on?
I hear police sirens, no, ambulance I think
People, people I know and love, are crying
I look around
And see nothing but a carpet full of blood and an empty gun
What happened?
What went wrong?
I can't remember, all I know is I'm gone
So many different things I wanted to do
But didn't take time to do them
I didn't think my life would be gone
In one single moment
I tell you now–
Live your life to the fullest
And cherish every moment

True Colors
by Jenna Juliano

As I sat sit, no movement or sound
Picked apart piece by piece, until the true me was finally unleashed
I wondered, am I still as beautiful now that you've seen my true colors?
Or am I just another object in this world
Unnoticed by the everyday creatures passing by
I'm no different than I was before
Still strong, confident, and secure
You've just studied me in a deeper way
Looked me over, inside and out
And have finally figured the true me out

Love Him Forever
by Charity Sier

Love him forever
Whatever it takes
Don't let him slip away
It won't be the same
He won't be there when you cry
He won't be there when you smile
He's slowly slipping away
There he goes, far, far away
Don't ever look away
He just might not
Be there the next day
Day in, day out
He's gone forever
That's why you should always
Love him forever

Swords and Shields
by Tim Bleecker

In the realm of life's broad battlefield
Let us wear the helm and bear the shield
But let us not be led astray
To take the sword and simply slay
For if we do naught but hate and kill
Then this may become our only will
And if we cannot lend a hand
To a fellow man and friend
And this while bearing mind to our defense
We shall see life as through a scratched lens
Seeing part and not the unblemished whole
Of ourselves: without knowledge to change or console

No More Promises, Daddy
by Marissa Nordman-Ernesti

You say I'm just as important
As the things that have gotten in the way
You say you love me all the time
But promise I wish you'd never say
You act like your absence
Hasn't affected me at all
But why is it when times get tough
I expect the most to fall?
I stay here broken
Waiting for you to follow through
But everyday there's a broken promise
And you expect that I trust you?

The Storm
by Michael Ramsey

The wind brushed against my face
Like an artist with a painting
Looking out to the ocean in all its grace
And the clouds in the sky waiting
The ocean, an array of light and color
Solitary beams of light penetrating the clouds
A lone soul I am, looking out in wonder
Listening to no sound
The sky becomes dark
The waves grow tall
Water on the beach leaves a mark
Suddenly seagulls begin to call
A faint noise arises in the distance
Little light escapes the clouds
I am calm in this instance
But suddenly the storm breaks loud
Light flashes across the sky
Thunder rumbles in its wake
The storm begins to die
And the ocean is now calm as a lake

3rd
Place

Julie Blum

Already a published author in her home state,
this high school freshman is a student of many interests,
including science, drama, and especially music.
Performing professionally since the age of thirteen,
Julie's specialty is the alto saxophone.
She has won numerous awards for her musical ability,
and now adds another in the field of creative writing.

Nocturnal Loss
by Julie Blum

I'll never know what hit me on that fated, summer night
Of glimmering stars and glistening tears
And each icy second seemed to stab with fervid fire, searing and sudden
Every appendage was shattered and I lay sprawled
Across the thin, bright yellow line with stunned, agonizing silence
As I waited for my existence to, at last, come to a doomed, impending end
The rusty, roaring, raging menace had materialized
No hesitation, no regret, cold and unfeeling
So now my heartbeat escalates, while expecting to plummet all too soon
Bringing its inevitable stop for all eternity
Fleeting visions arise; my meal waiting for me
Back in my pleasant sheltered den
My numerous siblings all crowded around, waiting
My parents concerned at my late return from foraging
Their bushy, ringed tails wrapped around their unscathed, furry bodies
As the indifferent killer speeds away from me
Laughing with a black heart, at the eventual halt of mine

2nd
Place

Brittany Short

Ninth grade student Brittany Short
is a First Sergeant
in her school's JROTC program.
With future aspirations
of becoming a special needs teacher,
Brittany also enjoys
singing and listening to music.
She lists writing
as her favorite pastime however,
and has worked hard to develop
the talent she naturally possesses.

Sweet Death
by Brittany Short

Look at her face you can see her pain
She can no longer sacrifice her soul for your pleasure
When you look in her eyes you see only your refection
She carries your love like a burden heavy upon her shoulders
She cannot think unless you say
You control her life
But her love for you is so strong that she cannot leave
She would rather die

Veronica Biblarz

Veronica is a student in the ninth grade
who has been blessed
with the gift of written expression.
Her ability to paint a mental picture
to which the reader can relate
is quite exceptional
as is evidenced in the poem
which captured our hearts.
It gives us great pleasure to present,
"Who's That?" by Veronica Biblarz,
our Editor's Choice Award Winner.

Editor's Choice Award

Who's That?
by Veronica Biblarz

Her frail body moves inside the captivity of age
She flashes a faint smile at the sweethearts out the window
The lipstick, stained on her teeth, enhances her beauty
Her gray hair falls into her eyes
She wisps it out, leaving the smell of perfume in the air
She sits, she waits, she lives day to day
Her white shoes ache her brittle body
She reaches to the molded candy dish to soothe her pain
Her weathered hands can still hold yours
The corner of her rickety wooden home is filled with memories
A picture of me, a picture of you, a picture of ... wait, who's that?
She has collections of everything
Someone's trash, was always her treasure
She now sleeps in the shadow of the world she is too small to face
Her kind voice will ring in the ears of loved ones through generations
The rocking chair in the den will bring sweet comfort in times of sorrow
She is free from captivity, instead, in an endless sea of warmth

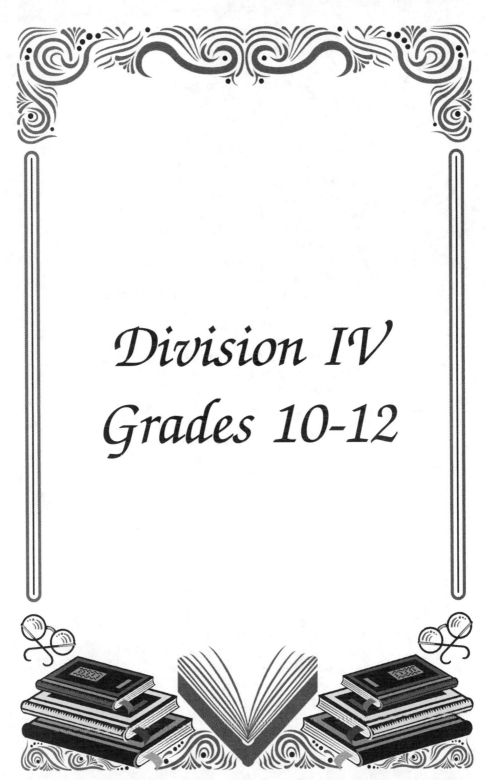

Division IV
Grades 10-12

Let's Make the World a Better Place
by Chloe Mapes

If you came across a person in danger
Would you just help that everyday stranger?
Or would you just pass by the way
And not even give them the time of day?
Too often people pass up the occasion
To become a hero in a mere situation
To earn the name hero, you don't need to be
The most well known note in life's symphony
A hero is someone who's courageous and bold
A hero can be someone who's not very old
But if you are not the bold and audacious
Let your thoughtfulness show by being gracious
The world needs people who are bold and altruistic
People, whose main concern is considered humanistic
People willing to risk their life
To save another's among all the strife
And just in case you forget
The traits of a hero cannot be bought
So walk out the door with arms of embrace
And let's make the world a better place

A Night's Catching Moment
by Mindy Glatfelter

The northern lights fill the sky
They make my worries soar and fly
The lights are bright as can be
They shine as far as I can see
My mind is blank as I stare
The northern lights are so rare
As I curl up and close my eyes
I realize my life is passing by
I need to stop and recognize
That life comes only in one size
So now I take my thoughts and dreams
Toward a lighted path that beams

The Conductress
by Erik Geiger

A pure romantic red
Cutable soft, like baked bread
You can be the symphony
And it will be the steady drum
If you say, "No", what will become?
It will burst, it'll run
Bleeding for your attention
So I will ask you this dire question
If you would be my symphony
I will be the steady drum
Now you see what is my heart
Pumping in and pumping out
Pierced it with your comforting smile
Cupped it in your warm hands
Will you leave me cold, standing
While I'm bleeding in those hands?

The Unmarked Grave
by Jenna Dennert

As I stare across the sky and sea
With my spirit wandering free
The waves crashing and churning
As grief keeps burning through me
The source of my pain is obviously clear
Since today was the death of somebody dear
My husband, my love, was sent far abroad
Where many have died, to meet up with God
Two soldiers came with faces so strained
To tell me the news that gave startling pain
"He died brave and true," I heard one of them say
As my world went dark and I started to sway
The lightning is flickering dim
The storm approaches with visage so grim
The rain, meanwhile, pounding, the echo
Resounding, the ocean escaping its brim
Sadly for me there's no trace of he
Who fought for the land of the brave
The world outside sleeps as I alone weep
For the man in the unmarked grave

Almost As Good As It Gets
by Amber McLaughlin

Playing through all the pain
The possibilities are endless
You aren't dreaming, this is your oasis
The longer you wait, the better it gets
It's our time now, the return of hope
We wish you were here, and then it'd be just right
The voices in our heads are in perfect harmony
No matter the twist of fate, keep a sense of balance
Turn left, turn right
We are ties that bind, let it all shine
In the end, do it for you or have a broken dream

The Times That Last
by Frank C. Figard IV

Storm clouds fade and light shines on me
Tears fill my eyes, happiness
Rays stream down as it dries the ground
Warmth grows inside, I'm a mess
Memories return to heal me
Sadness becomes my strange past
Forgetting most of, most of my unknown
Remembering the times that last
I look out my window, smiling
I'm free of pain and lies
All around me the flowers grow
The feeling of regret dies
Memories return to heal me
Sadness becomes my strange past
Forgetting most of, most of my unknown
Remembering the times that last
Now that I'm happy, I'm free
No sorrow to depress me
Just high expectations to find
Life's great, I finally see

Accident of Instability
by Samantha Curran

All this time I thought you were my intimate passion
My heart beats in a denying fashion
Burning broken brittle heart, a devil's attraction
A frosty drift through my heart you were
With the everlasting memories, I wish could be a blur
Meaninglessly left me cold and lonely
For a competition for what seems to be boney
Can't compete with the memory
Of something I'll never be
You took advantage of me
Instigating for what I thought seemed to be real
You were after me for only my appeal
The truth is hidden between all these buried lies
Torn at the heart, with inconceivable feelings that can't be seen through my eyes
Pushed, pulled, shoved, abused emotionally by you
On purpose may it not be
But your simple accident and my instability
Back and forth, confused and abused
An undefined love has caught me by surprise of you

Loneliness
by Brianna Albert

Who knew I could be so lonely
In a crowded room with everybody?
Who knew sorrow would be my worst
Enemy and my best friend?
How can my heart feel this way
When I love and care for so many?
Who knew I could feel so empty inside?
It is like someone is squeezing my heart
I hope these feelings aren't around the bend
Who knew ... loneliness

Questions
by Toby Neal

Why, how, these questions are almost never truly answered
Why is war allowed to walk freely? Some say the reason is unfairness
Then though, tell me in your own words, unfairness
What I may think is unfair may not be what you think is unfair
I think it is unfair that innocent people are killed; do you?
Some say that those "animals" are not innocent at all
That, in fact, they are Iraqis and are getting what they deserve
They even tell themselves that those "animals" are scapegoats
Sacrificing themselves so that "we" may live a better life
However, who is to say that "our" life is better
Because of the death of those "animals"
And if life was better
Who is to say that "we" want to live a better life at their expense
Why, how, these questions are almost never truly answered
Everyone thinks differently, everyone expresses themselves in different ways
Everyone has different answers
That is the reason these questions are almost never truly answered
Any questions?

Consideration
by Adam Lidgett

How is a man considered a man?
Is it put on him by his peers?
Deemed on him by the society surrounding him?
But shouldn't a man be more of himself
If he not succumbs to the pressures of those who surround him?
A man should be considered on
If he forgives the ones around him
And holds himself higher than the rest
But at the same time
Not considering himself as he is
That is what should be considered ...
A man

Fate
by Matthew Nielsen

The trepidation of fate
The desperate scrambling, struggling to decide
To devise a curve or mark in life
The ceaseless fight to have more, get more
Greed is natural, it comes with learning more
The uneducated do labor, and receive a pittance
But at least they live
The rich hire servants to clean the dirt from their houses
And go to a plush office to get more
With learning comes knowledge better left unexplored
Studies that destroy, maim, slaughter in the process
All to alter fate to man's liking
Knowledge isn't evil itself, but how it's used can be
We all desire to have the upper hand, some no matter the consequences
But where are we in the end?

Heaven's Aficionado
by Brittney Behr

The sky has no beginning
No middle, no end
She cannot be touched, or altered by any human hand
I stand on the shoreline, admiring my all-seeing friend
Wondering what dance she plans to attend
Will she cotillion with crimson?
Perhaps beguine with blue?
Will I witness a shy polonaise with purple?
Oh, how I wish she would courante with coral!
But whatever her choice, I promised I would stand
And watch her, so wonderfully open, and majestically grand
I realized then that if my life were to suddenly end
My wish would be to take her hand
And dance, and dance
For all of the aficionados like me I left back on land

Chivalry Is Dead
by Samantha Labate

Forgotten dreams
Thoughtless words
Bring the world down on young disasters
We are all used and abused
And finally broken by fears
Temptations and the thirst for love
Break even the strong
Chivalry is dead
No longer are kind words spoken
People are only controlled by lust and money
Thoughts and feelings are bottled up inside
Only to fester and boil
One wrong move can set anyone off
It is how hate and murder are brought to existence
And chivalry is dead

My Heaven
by Jenny Thompson

I once had a dream where I soared through the sky
All of my life I had been waiting to fly
The wind in my hair and the ground spread below
Into blue sky I was yearning to go
Everything I knew was down there on the ground
But the people I loved were too small to be found
I smiled at the Earth, then flew to the sun
The wind and I, we had become one
Although this dream passed, as all dreams do
I still pray that is the place I will one day go to

Don't Go
by Nicole Longenecker

I know you're old enough
To work through the hard thoughts
I know you're ready to leave
But I just can't believe
How fast time flew
Now I just feel so blue
I just want to say
Please don't go away
Some people just let go
But I can't let go
You've been there for all my life
Now my heart is being stabbed by a knife
I can't believe you're gone
Now I'm all alone
I wish you could come back
But you can't come back
And some day we'll meet again
And that day will wash away my pain

Thanksgiving
by Jessica Brooks

There's a box in an alley; it's late November
Inside there's a man who's hungry and shivering
He has no food, nor family, or pride
But today he's thankful to be alive
A young girl with cancer is waiting for a cure
And she's asking how could God do this to her?
But her parents never once leave her side
Today she is thankful for all the love in her life
Somewhere a junkie is getting out of rehab
He's going to try so hard to get his life back
He's going to work and pray, and break his addictions
Today he's thankful for all his second chances
There's a soldier halfway 'round the world
Wondering if he'll ever meet his baby girl
But he's proud of what he's doing, keeping the rest of us safe
So we can have Thanksgiving dinner and enjoy the holidays

Her Hero
by Emily De Fore

It all took place on that day in September
And I will remember that face now and forever
I will never forget those men and women who stood up tall
Who went without regret, even when buildings start to fall
A little girl was packed down tight
But she held on to her world, she wouldn't go down without a fight
Those brave, brave men, who risked their lives
Said, "Honey don't fret, you will be alright"
He took her hand, trembling with barely a pulse
Said, "Honey you can make it, just stay close"
Four years later, on September 11, 2005
They celebrated saving her because she is still alive
Her heroes stood before her and she didn't know what to say
But her father pushed her forward, offering a hand to shake
However, those men would not accept
They wrapped her with a hug
And said, "Honey don't forget, when life gets hard, stay tough"

I'm Here For You
by Jasmine Ford

It must be hard waking up in the morning
Knowing he's not there
Your mind racing everywhere
Wondering what went wrong
Why life seems like a sad song
If there is a God, why did He let him go
When He knew I would miss him so?
I don't know why He let him go
But this I know
God sends us trials to make us grow
He knows you can't do it on your own
That's why He sent you me
Someone to lean on, cry on, and depend on
Someone who knows what it feels like
To have the ground ripped up underneath you
I know what it feels like, but what can you do?
You come to me, sorrow and all
For I will never let you fall

I Remember
by Ruiyu Wu

I remember a day, a day in the past
When I did not know the feeling of love
But then I had met you, and felt my heart swell
And you fluttered away, away like a dove
I remember a thought, a thought of my mind
I dreamed you were here, here in my world
I reached out to you; I reached for your heart
You reached back to me, and my mind whirled
I remember a time, a time of a feel
That time you were angry at my mistake
I cried and pleaded for you to forgive
But you would not change, for your own sake
I remember that day, that day in the rain
The day that you left, walked out of my sight
I cried, and I cried, and cried my eyes dry
But I could not bring you back in my life

Never Say Forever
by Ashlee Bartman

Never say, "I love you"
If you don't really care
Never talk about feelings
If they aren't really there
Never hold my hand
If you're going to break my heart
Never say you're going to
If you don't plan to start
Never look into my eyes
If you all speak are lies
Never say, "Hi"
If you really mean goodbye
If you really mean forever
Then say you will try
Never say forever
Because forever makes me cry

Amy
by Casey Hubert

It was such a date
When cancer took her fate
Flushed face
A loss in the human race
Better place
Solemn November day
The trees began to sway
Crying faces
Better places
No traces
A loss of soul
That was God's goal
To make us realize
The size
Of the prize
We had lost

Waiting For Freedom
by Tenya Thurston

Not a day goes by without fear, without hunger, or death
I wince at the sound of gunshots
And tremble at the thought that I may be next
The food is detestable and small
Our water is polluted and dirty
Despite these facts, I eat and drink for my survival
Every night I lie in bed, I think of my dead family
Asking for their protection, so that I may live on for their sake
Every time I close my eyes
Wishing, waiting, simply waiting
Each time I wake another has died
I wanted to cry for them, but I have no tears left to cry
I work and work, with hope that today won't be my last
As the German soldiers walk by, a cold chill runs down my spine
Within myself a cold hatred has been bottled up, unable to be unleashed
I hide all emotion; both sorrow, hatred, and anguish
But I feel something coming nearer and nearer with each day
It is something glorious, I know it
Until then, I'm here waiting
Simply waiting for freedom

What's Missing?
by Rena Pereira

You look up and down, left to right, can't figure out what's missing
I lay in bed tossing and turning, still don't know what's missing
I feel my heartbeat racing, when I hear your name
I still can't figure out what's missing; at the end of the day, I still wonder
It still drives me crazy, I feel mindless, empty-headed
But I look right in front of me, I was shocked, I was missing you
My friend, my supporter, my treasure ... You

Delirious
by Ana Lucia de Hoyos

Her eyes fluttered open at the sound of an ambulance
She turned her head slowly to the clock sitting on her nightstand
2:58
Sighing, she turned her head to face the ceiling once again
Uneasy thoughts kept her awake
She could hear the breathing of her sister, the groaning of her brother
The beating of her own heart
All she could think of was
How she could make it seem normal, how to forget it
How she should react, how she would react
She turned to look at the clock again
2:59
She looked back up, annoyed by the way time seemed to slow down
Again she tried to sleep, this time closing her eyes, trying harder
The same questions came to her train of thought
She opened her eyes, frustrated
Perhaps these questions would be easier to answer
If she knew the problems, the situation
She then glanced at the clock
2:58

3rd
Place

Krystina Kelly

Born in Russia, Krystina now calls America home.
When she isn't reading works by her favorite poet, Robert Frost,
she enjoys helping children as a volunteer at a community day camp.
She has won numerous writing contests,
and takes a philosophical approach to poetry,
the function of which she maintains,
is to help us all feel a little less alone in the world.

Anointed
by Krystina Kelly

Take these unblessed ashes and place them on your forehead
Anoint your sons and daughters with this dust
Hold this blackened Eucharist on your tongue
Construct a prayer for those who had no time to speak
A song for those whose lives remain unsung
Recall, as you inhale their smoke
The world, the way it was, before you woke
A yesterday when drums and bagpipes called us not to funerals
When snowy wafts of ticker tape announced a glad parade
To celebrate the "boys of summer" in their hour of glory
Give faithful homage to a game well played
By rules that every schoolchild agreed must be upheld
For that remembered world our parents made
These ashes are communion, or flesh and steel ignited
When a world, no longer young, witnessed unleashed terror
That drew our city's blood
A pain, that swallowed, made us stand as one
Take these unblessed ashes and place them on your forehead
Anoint your sons and daughters with this dust

Jeffrey Wellman

Jeffrey is a high school senior
who credits his English teacher
for his involvement in poetry.
What began as a poetry journal assignment,
has now become an outlet for personal expression.
His winning entry is based on his observations of life's cycles,
which sadly, often lead to decline in later years.

Old House
by Jeffrey Wellman

He became an old house
The front porch railing with its missing spindles
That made up his worn smile
The stiffened joints that echoed the creaking stairs
As he slowly ambled up to bed
And the vacant eyes with their shades closed
Detached from the living world
The yard and flower beds were left unkempt
Since he hadn't trimmed his beard in years
His furnace broke the day his wife died
The cold crept in and filled his bones
With a terminal ache and longing
Now all that's left is the leaky roof
Where the rain soaks in
And the memories seep out

Alexandra Winzeler

A senior in high school,
Alexandra has a flair for creative writing.
Family is obviously very important to her
and through her natural descriptive ability,
she is able to draw us,
as readers,
into a poignant and personal scene,
and share with us
some very warm and relatable moments.

The Geography of Genetics
by Alexandra Winzeler

I hover in the valleys of your breathing
Praying and worrying the pause will stretch forever
Your skin is worn soft, like a stone
Against which waters' currents have run
Among the disinfectant of a hospital
The sigh of tulip soap lingers with you
In the solemn solidarity, I watch you sleep
Where am I in the map of your face?
There — over the wave of a cheekbone and across closed eyes
I am made of everything that came before: I am made of you
I once found it inconceivable that I would someday be
A teenager, a woman , a mother —
But the concept of time now fits within my mind
Someday I will be worn, soft like a storm-tossed stone
And a grandchild will watch over while I sleep
Surveying the map of my features, searching for her place
And while waiting in the valleys of my breathing
She will come to the crest of my cheekbone, the curve of my closed eye
And recognize herself
She doesn't know it, but in that moment, she has also found you
And everything that came before
Ringing somewhere deep and distant
Like a song she had never heard with her ears
But which felt so familiar in her heart

Index

of

Authors

Index of Authors

Index of Authors

Index of Authors

Index of Authors

Brilliance
Price List

Initial Copy 32.95

Additional Copies 24.00

Please Enclose $6 Shipping/Handling Each Order

Check or Money Order Payable to:

The America Library of Poetry
P.O. Box 978
Houlton, Maine 04730

Must specify book title and author

Please Allow 21 Days For Delivery

THE AMERICA
LIBRARY OF POETRY

www.libraryofpoetry.com
Email: generalinquiries@libraryofpoetry.com

Poetry On the Web

See Your Poetry Online!

This is a special honor reserved exclusively for our published poets.
Now that your work has been forever set in print,
why not share it with the world at www.libraryofpoetry.com

At the America Library of Poetry,
our goal is to showcase quality writing in such a way
as to inspire others to broaden their literary horizons,
and we can think of no better way to reach people around the world
than by featuring poetic offerings like yours on our global website.

Since we already have your poem in its published format,
all you need to do is copy the information from the form below on
a separate sheet of paper, and return it with a $6 posting fee.
This will allow us to display your poetry
on the internet for one full year.

Author's Name _____

Poem Title _____

Book Title _____ *Brilliance* _____

Mailing Address _____

City _____ State _____ Zip Code _____

E-mail Address _____

Check or Money Order in the amount of $6 payable to:
The America Library of Poetry
P.O. Box 978
Houlton, Maine 04730